THE

ATHOLL

GLENS

THE ATHOLL
GLENS

A personal survey of the Atholl Glens

for mountainbikers and walkers

by

Peter D. Koch-Osborne

© P. D. Koch-Osborne 1993
ISBN 1 85284 121 4

First Published 1993
Reprinted 1999

British Library Cataloguing-in-Publication Data.
A catalogue record for this book
is available from the British Library.

Mountains are the beginning
and the end of all
natural scenery.

John Ruskin.

Cover pictures:-   Gleann Taitneach
Loch Ordie

Index

Introduction

Access to the tracks on the following pages can rarely be regarded as an absolute right by the cyclist or walker. Almost all land is private and it is often only the good nature of the owners that allows us to travel unhindered over the land. In Scottish law the term trespass implies nuisance or damage. In practice sensible conduct removes any possibility of nuisance. Respect the grouse season (12th August to 10th December) and deer stalking (stags: 1 July to 20th October, and hinds: 21st October to 15th February). Your author has not once met with any animosity in meeting gamekeepers. Only good conduct will ensure continued access. Cyclists - stay on the trail and slow down!

Conservation of the wild areas of Scotland is of paramount importance. Users of this guide must appreciate that the very ground over which you walk or cycle will be damaged if care is not taken. Please do not use a bike on soft peat paths and tread carefully on other than a stony track. Many of the tracks are themselves an eyesore. So-called development can cause irreparable damage. Make sure, as walkers and cyclists we encourage the conservation of our wilderness areas without the pressure of our activities causing further damage. In publishing this book great responsibility is placed on you, the reader, to respect the needs of the region. If all you need is exercise - go to a sports centre! If you appreciate the unique qualities of these wild places they are yours to enjoy - with care! Careless conduct not only damages what we seek to enjoy, but equally seriously gives landowners good reason to restrict access.

<u>The Maps</u> on the following pages provide sufficient detail for exploration of the glens but the O.S. Landranger maps of the region should also be used if the geographical context of the area is to be fully appreciated. These maps, and the knowledge of their proper use are essential if a longer tour or cross country route is to be undertaken.

<u>The mountain bike</u> has in your author's opinion been badly named. It does not belong on the high tops but is ideal in the glens covering about twice the distance of the average walker, quietly. It allows full appreciation of the surroundings and makes possible further exploration into the wilderness especially on short winter days. The bike must be a well maintained machine complete with a few essential spares as a broken bike miles from anywhere can be serious. Spare gear is best carried in a light rucksack or in good quality panniers. Front panniers help distribute weight and prevent 'wheelies'. Heavy rucksacks upset balance, cause backache, and put more weight onto one's already battered posterior! The brightly coloured 'high profile' image of mountainbiking, hyped up by glossy magazines is, in your author's opinion, unsuited to the remote glens. These wild areas are sacred and deserve a more inconspicuous approach.

<u>Clothing</u> for the off-road cyclist is an important consideration. Traditional road cycling gear is unsuitable. High ankle trainers are best in summer and lightweight summer walking boots are best for winter cycling. A variety of thin or fleece 'longs' with a thermal inner layer keep legs warm in any season, even shorts have been seen in July! A man-made thermal 'top' or T-shirt with

one, (or two in winter) fleece zip jackets will keep your trunk warm. Avoid cotton at all costs - it is too absorbent. The wearing of a helmet is personal choice - a definite 'yes' if road cycling - freedom versus safety off-road. It depends how and where you ride. In any event a helmet cover and head-band will be needed in winter - or a balaclava - also good ski gloves. Protection against exposure should be as for mountain walking. Remember many glens are as high as English hilltops. Also include full water-proofs in your pack.

Clothing for the walker in the glens is much as above, substituting the 'skid lid' for heavier boots and possibly gaiters. An extra layer, or heavier waterproof jacket should be taken for the higher passes and if mountain summits are to be included. In winter, conditions above (and sometimes in) the glens necessitate specialized gear and experience - beyond the scope of this book.

Safety and conduct are two important con-siderations. Never be without a good map, this book (!), a whistle (and knowledge of its proper use), compass, emergency rations, and spare clothing. Word of your planned route should be left together with your estimated time of arrival. The bothies must be left tidy - with firewood where appropri-ate - for the next visitor. Don't be too proud to remove someone else's litter. It should not be necessary to repeat the Country Code and the Mountain Bike Code. The true lover of the wild places needs peace and space - not rules and regulations. With common sense and manners there is room for the walker, cyclist and landowner!

River crossings are a major consideration when planning long through routes in wild regions of Scotland. It must be remembered that snowmelt from the high mountains can turn what is a fordable burn in early morning into a raging torrent by mid afternoon. Walkers should hold on to each other, taking turns to move. Rivers can be easier to cross with a bike, as the bike can be moved, brakes applied, and used to assist balance as feet are moved. The procedure is to remove boots and socks, replace boots only, make sure you can't drop anything and cross – ouch !! Drain boots well, dry your feet, and the theory is that your still dry socks will help to warm your feet up. Snowmelt is cold enough to hurt. Choose a wide shallow place to cross and above all don't take risks.

Ascents on a bike should be tackled slowly in a very low gear, sitting down to help the rear wheel grip. Bar end extensions help. Standing on the pedals causes wheel slip, erosion of the track and is tiring. Pushing a bike, especially if loaded, is no fun and often the result of starting the climb too fast, in the wrong gear, standing up, or all three!

Descents on a bike can be exhilarating, but a fast descent is hard on both bike and rider, and can be dangerous (see 'helmets'!). If your rear wheel is locked this causes erosion. It is also ill-mannered (at best) towards others to ride too fast.

Last but not least I make no apology for repeating my request for good manners. We walk and cycle in what is a working environment, however wild or desolate it may sometimes appear. Smile and be pleasant - the guy you meet may own the entire view!

9

The Maps

The maps are drawn to depict the features most relevant to the explorer of the glens. North is at the top of each map and all maps, apart from introductory section maps and detail maps, are to the same scale :- 1km or 0.6miles being shown on each map. An attempt has been made to present the maps in a pictorially interesting way. A brief explanation of the various features is set out below:-

Tracks:-

One of the prime objects of these books is to grade the tracks according to roughness. This information is essential to the cyclist and useful to the walker. With due respect to the O.S. one "other road, drive or track" can take twice as long to cycle as another, yet both may be depicted in the same way. Your author's method of grading is set out below:-

metalled road. Not too many fortunately, public roads are generally included only to locate the start of a route.

good track, hardly rutted, nearly as fast as a road to cycle on but can be tedious to walk far on. Most are forest tracks.

the usual rutted estate track, rough but all rideable on a mountain bike. Not too tedious to walk on.

rough, very rutted track, nearly all rideable. Either very stony or boggy or overgrown. Can be rough even to walk.

walker's path. Only part rideable but not usually advised with a bike. May be used as part of a 'through' bike route.

10

Relief is depicted in two ways. The heavy lines depict main mountain ridges, summits and spurs thus:—

Contour lines are also used, at 50m intervals, up to about 600m. This adds shape to the glens as mapped and gives an idea of how much climbing is involved. Reference to gradient profiles at the start of each section compares the various routes.

Crags are shown thus:— with major areas of scree dotted.

Rivers generally 'uncrossable' are shown as two lines whilst small streams or burns are shown using a single line. Note, great care is needed crossing larger burns and rivers. Falling in can cause embarrassment at best, exposure or even drowning at worst. Please don't take risks— besides, you'd get this book wet!!

loch or lochan

Buildings and significant ruins are shown as:.......

Bridges are rather obviously shown thus:— with an indication of type of construction to assist location.

Trees are so numerous your author wishes there were an easier way of drawing them but there isn't!! etc...

11

Atholl Glens – North

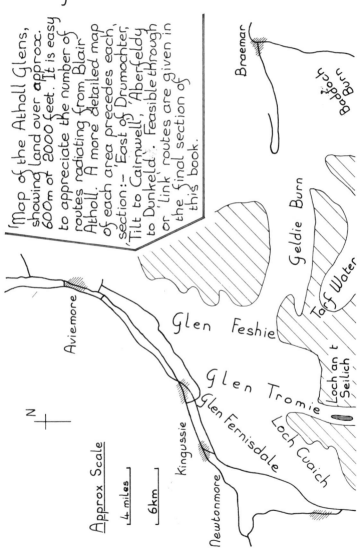

Map of the Atholl Glens, showing land over approx. 600m or 2000 feet. It is easy to appreciate the number of routes radiating from Blair Atholl. A more detailed map of each area precedes each section:- 'East of Drumochter', 'Tilt to Cairnwell', 'Aberfeldy to Dunkeld'. Feasible through or 'link' routes are given in the final section of this book.

Braemar

Baddoch Burn

Geldie Burn

Tarf Water

Glen Feshie

Aviemore

N

Glen Tromie

Glen Fernisdale

Loch an t Seilich

Loch Cuaich

Kingussie

Newtonmore

Approx Scale

4 miles

6 km

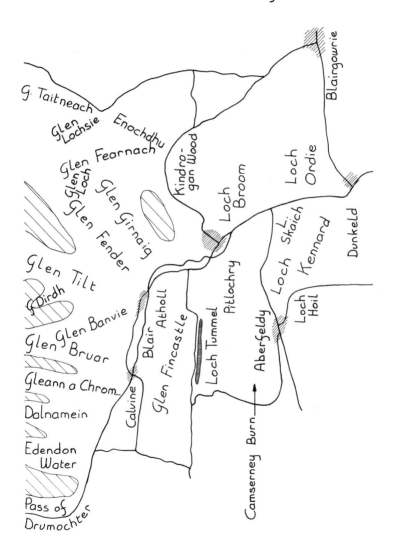

East of Drumochter

Access:—Access to the East of Drumochter district is directly off the A9. Virtually all the routes in this section start within a stones throw of this major road. The area is also one of the few where the railway may be used to advantage both in getting there in the first place and for returning to the start of 'point to point' routes. The old A9, now a minor road or just a strip of abandoned tarmac should be used for local access. Most of the world passes this area by at 70mph. Slow down, and fully appreciate what these remote glens have to offer.

Accommodation:— Blair Atholl provides everything from hotels to campsites and there are two Youth Hostels, at Pitlochry and Kingussie. There is a distinct lack of winter campsites as most close, and not much of anything at all between Calvine and Newtonmore. The Tourist Information Centres are in Pitlochry and Kingussie, Blair Atholl would benefit from one also. The Blair Atholl area is usually very busy in summer. The other three seasons are best!

Geographical Features:— East of Drumochter lies a vast area of rounded high moors clad in heather. The woods around Blair Atholl, cut with deep ravines and fast flowing rivers, provide a dramatic contrast with the remainder of the area. The dams and hydro-electric scheme centred on Loch an t- Seilich and Loch Cuaich provides man-made interest and is responsible for the construction of some of the tracks. The area has the A9 as its northern, western and southern boundaries and the east of the district is bounded by Glen Tromie, Glen Bruar and Glen Banvie.

Mountains:— An area of high moors is dominated by Beinn Dearg, east of Glen Bruar. The area is a 'tame' version of the great Cairngorm heights providing somewhat tedious walking across its pathless tops combined with long distances. The glens provide much greater interest

East of Drumochter Routes 1

Glen Tromie

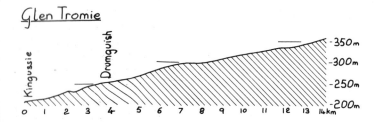

Glen Fernisdale

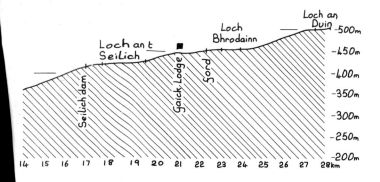

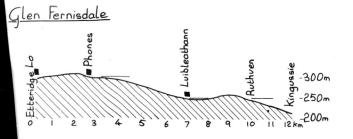

18

which is a good excuse for concentrating exploration of this region at low level, besides - it's easier!

Rivers:– The minor rivers are not all they seem as water is used in the hydro-electric schemes of the district. Many rivers are therefore smaller and easier to cross than the map indicates. From Edendon Water south all rivers drain into the Garry although water is diverted via Loch Ericht, Loch Rannoch and Loch Tummel for power generation before entering River Garry. River crossings are not a problem apart from a major ford near Gaick Lodge in Glen Tromie, making Glen Tromie to Edendon Water a route for a dry summer. Please don't take chances here!!

Forests:– The woodlands around Blair Atholl provide superb variety of both conifer and deciduous trees, have spent many days exploring in their company. J north of Blair Atholl Balvain Wood, a commercial pl ation, is constantly changing due to felling operati Here unceasing noise from the A9 spoils the lower trac

Lochs:– The largest and most dramatic is Loch an t-S enlarged by a hydro dam, as is the second loch in district - Loch Cuaich. Loch Bhrodainn and Loch an squeezed into the Tromie/Edendon Water watershed Gaick Pass) were the reason for General Wade s ing the Drumochter route for his road, the only alternative being Glen Bruar and the very e Minigaig Pass. A couple of pleasant lochans found in Glen Fernisdale.

Emergency:– Most glens have occupied houses the public roads. Bruar and Gaick Lodges are Shelters and bothies are noted on the detail ma

Public telepones (apart	Drumguish	795995
from the obvious) are	Dalnaspidal	645733
situated at :–	Calvine	804659

... these are O.S. grid references
   – not 'phone numbers!!

Loch Cuaich

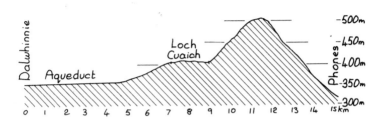

Edendon Water

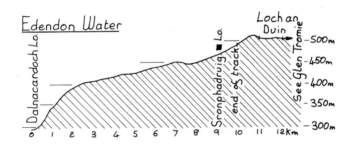

Dalnamein

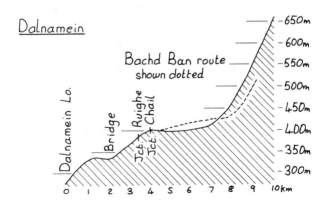

East of Drumochter Routes 3

Gleann a Chrombaidh

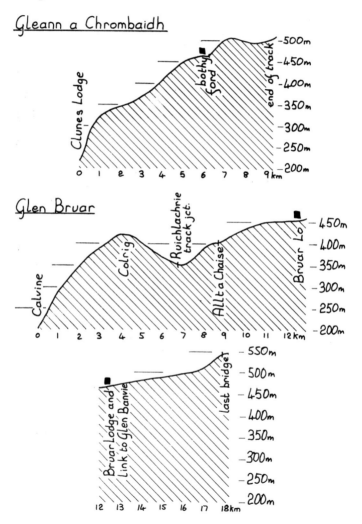

Clunes Lodge — bothy — ford — end of track

500m, 450m, 400m, 350m, 300m, 250m, 200m

0 1 2 3 4 5 6 7 8 9 km

Glen Bruar

Calvine — Colrig — Ruichlachrie track jct. — Allt a Chaise — Bruar Lo

450m, 400m, 350m, 300m, 250m, 200m

0 1 2 3 4 5 6 7 8 9 10 11 12 km

Bruar Lodge and Link to Glen Banvie — last bridge

550m, 500m, 450m, 400m, 350m, 300m, 250m, 200m

12 13 14 15 16 17 18 km

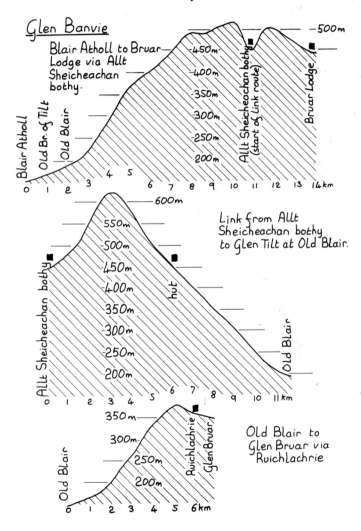

Glen Banvie

Blair Atholl to Bruar Lodge via Allt Sheicheachan bothy.

Link from Allt Sheicheachan bothy to Glen Tilt at Old Blair.

Old Blair to Glen Bruar via Ruichlachrie

21

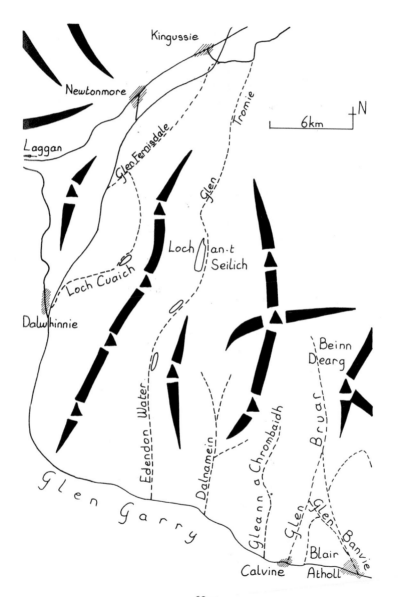

Some glens are suitable only for walkers and some are more suitable for mountainbikers. Glen Tromie is, in the author's humble opinion a mountainbiker's glen as the "track" is metalled almost to the Hydro Electric dam at Loch an t-Seilich. However if the "through route" to Edendon Water is planned a bike would have to be wheeled or carried past Loch an Duin for about 2km or 1½ miles. The best plan may be to cycle to the head of the glen and explore from there on foot. Beyond Gaick Lodge there is a major ford and a beautiful waterfall up a side-glen. Glen Tromie also leads to the Minigaig Pass -a high mountain route (outside the scope of this book) to Glen Bruar. The smooth tarmac is either alien to the walker or purist mountainbiker or a godsend to the cyclist who's posterior needs a rest from rough tracks, indeed a racing bike could be used as far as the dam. The Hydro Electric scheme, a bit of inspired pre-war thinking (when "green" was just a colour!) is of interest as water bound for Edendon Water and the River Garry is diverted into the Tromie (which is bound for the Spey), again diverted by tunnel to Cuaich and aqueduct over the R. Truim to Loch Ericht, thence via Loch Tummel back into the Garry. The water passes through several power stations. The result in environmental terms is some undersized rivers, a few dams, aqueducts and pipes, surely better than polluted skies with holes in the ozone layer or potential disasters around the country in the shape of nuclear power stations. So much for the environment - but this is a guide book and here are some distances from Kingussie :-

Seilich Dam	18 km	11 m
Gaick Lodge	21 km	13 m
Loch an Duin (end of track)	28 km	17 m
Sronphadruig Lo.(bothy) (via Edendon Water)	30 km	19 m
Dalnacardoch Lodge (on the A9)	38 km	24 m

There is no shelter in Glen Tromie.

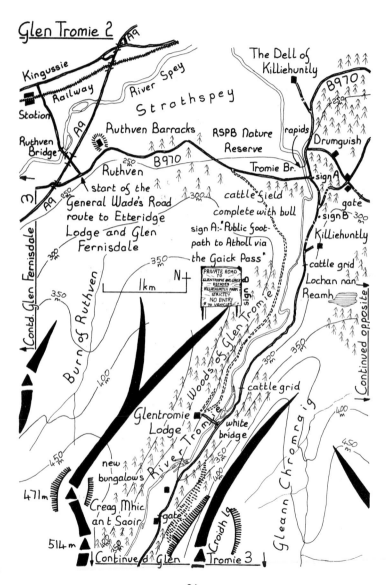

Glen Tromie 2

Kingussie

Railway

River Spey

Strothspey

Station

The Dell of Killiehuntly

B970

Ruthven Barracks

RSPB Nature Reserve

rapids

Drumguish

Ruthven Bridge

250

B970

Ruthven

Tromie Br.

sign A

gate

A9

250

start of the
General Wade's Road
route to Etteridge
Lodge and Glen
Fernisdale

300 m

cattle field
complete with bull

sign A:- "Public foot-
path to Atholl via
the Gaick Pass"

sign B

300 m

Killiehuntly

cattle grid

Lochan nan Reamh

350 m

N

1km

PRIVATE ROAD
TO
GLENTROMIE AND GAICK
ESTATES
KILLIEHUNTLY PARK
STRICTLY
NO ENTRY
TO VEHICLES
sign

Contd Glen Fernisdale

300 m

350 m

Burn of Ruthven

400 m

350 m

300 m

Woods of Glen Tromie

350 m

Continued opposite

400 m

cattle grid

Glentromie Lodge

white bridge

River Tromie

Gleann Chromaig

400 m

450 m

new bungalows

350 m

Creag Mhic an t'Saoir

400 m

450 m

gate

Croidh Le

471m

514 m

Continued Glen

Tromie 3

24

▲ 468m

↑ Continued Glen Tromie 2 ↑

450 m

Sron na Gaoithe

Lyna-berack Lodge

Lynaberack

cattle grid

▲ 521m

450 m

Lynacragan (ruin)

The birchwoods of lower Glen Tromie give way to wild moors as the Minigaig Pass route forks to the east. The "track" continues as smooth tarmac.

350 m

NO footbridge (marked on O.S. maps)

Clach mheall

▲ 626 m

River Tromie

400 350 350

695m

400 m

footbridge

400 m

The Allt Bhrandam diverts water to the Seilich-Cuaich hyd-ro system

N

1 km

450 m

cattle grid

400 m

400 m

girder bridge

Allt

X-X (See Glen Tromie 4) is a rough path giving superb views from the high level track at Y worth the diversion when heading north

Bhran dam

450 m

400 m

Y

footbridge

X

MINIGAIG

↓ Continued Glen Tromie 4 ↓

Glen Tromie 4.

↑ Contd. Glen Tromie 3 ↑

The environs of Loch an t-Seilich and Gaick Lodge are dramatic. The Lodge lies on the flat, half mile wide glen floor whilst to the south the glen narrows into the steep sided avalanche prone gorge of Loch an Duin which put the main routes north several km west over the longer Drumochter Pass.

The Loch an t Seilich dam sends water via a tunnel to Loch Cuaich for power generation. Note the elaborate circular salmon 'ladder'.

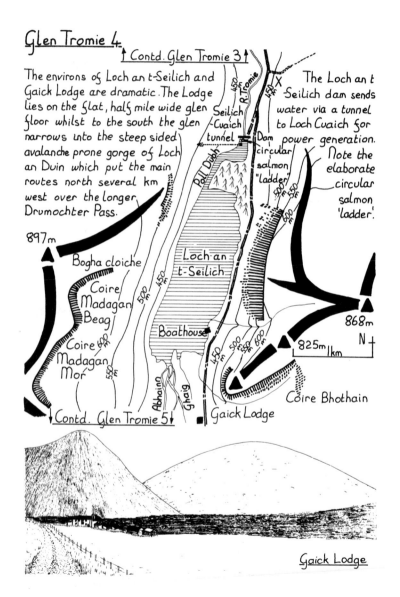

897m

Bogha cloiche

Coire Madagan Beag

Coire Madagan Mor

Loch an t-Seilich

Boathouse

Seilich Cuaich tunnel

Allt Diúb

Dam circular salmon "ladder"

R.Tromie

450

450

500

550

600

868m

825m

N

1km

Coire Bhothain

Abhainn Ghaig

Gaick Lodge

↓ Contd. Glen Tromie 5 ↓

Gaick Lodge

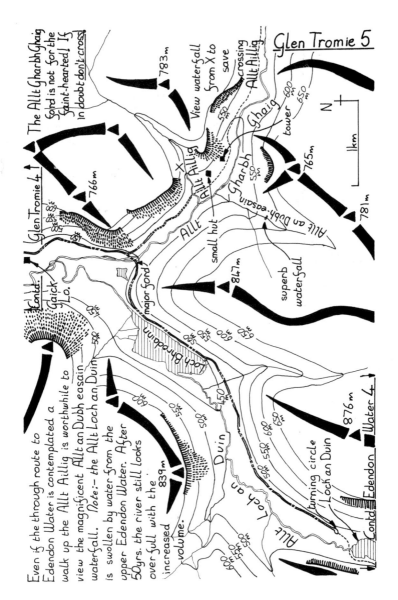

Glen Fernisdale 1

Glen Fernisdale to the Milton Burn traces General Wade's route from Glen Truim to Strathspey which short-cuts the A9 and railway. Although a point-to-point route, cyclists can turn it into a 'circular' by using the abandoned A9 and the B9150/A86 through Newtonmore so avoiding the dreaded A9 completely. The country through which one passes is more wild than a glance at the O.S. map suggests and the highlight of the trip has to be an original 'General Wade's' bridge. There is shelter near the Milton Burn. The one way trip from Kingussie to the A9 at Etteridge Lodge is 12km (7m). Note the 'crossing route' from the A9 via Phones over to Loch Cuaich, a new track which extends the off-road alternative to the A9 south to Dalwhinnie. The train can be used between Kingussie and Dalwhinnie.

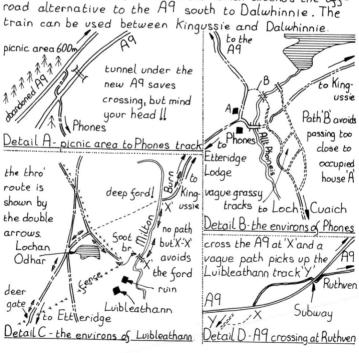

picnic area 600m

abandoned A9

A9

tunnel under the new A9 saves crossing, but mind your head !!

Phones

Detail A - picnic area to Phones track

to the A9

B

A

to Phones

Allt Phones

to Kingussie

Path 'B' avoids passing too close to occupied house 'A'

vague grassy tracks to Loch Cuaich

Detail B - the environs of Phones

the thro' route is shown by the double arrows.

Lochan Odhar

deer gate

to Etteridge

deep ford!

Milton Burn

Scot br.

to Kingussie

no path but 'X-X' avoids the ford

fence

ruin

Luibleathann

Detail C - the environs of Luibleathann.

to Etteridge Lodge

cross the A9 at 'X' and a vague path picks up the Luibleathann track 'Y'

A9

Y

X

Ruthven

Subway

Detail D - A9 crossing at Ruthven

28

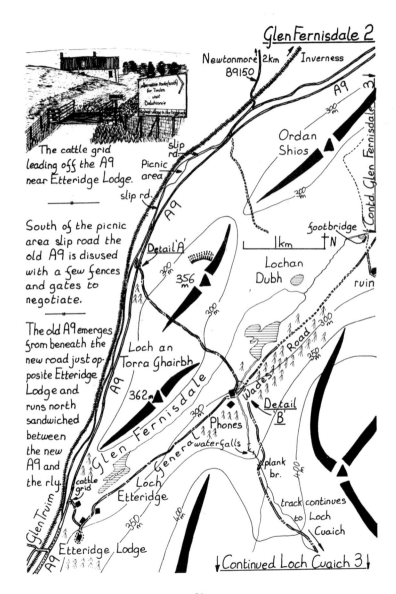

Newtonmore 2km Inverness
B9150

A9

Ordan
Shios

300 m

300

Contd. Glen Fernisdale 3

slip rd.

Picnic area

slip rd.

A9

footbridge

N

1km

Detail 'A'

300 m

356 m

Lochan Dubh

ruin

300

300

300

Wade's Road

300

350

South of the picnic area slip road the old A9 is disused with a few fences and gates to negotiate.

The old A9 emerges from beneath the new road just opposite Etteridge Lodge and runs north sandwiched between the new A9 and the rly.

Loch an Torra Ghairbh

362 m

Glen Fernisdale

General

Phones

waterfalls

Wade's

Detail B

plank br.

400

300

A9

cattle grid

Loch Etteridge

350

400

track continues to Loch Cuaich

Glen Truim

A9

Etteridge Lodge

↓ _Continued Loch Cuaich 3_ ↓

The cattle grid leading off the A9 near Etteridge Lodge.

29

Glen Fernisdale 3

This section of the route from Ruthven to Wades bridge is slow going and care is needed in routefinding. Refer to detail sketches C and D.

KINGUSSIE

School

Station

Ruthven Barracks

Bridge of Ruthven

Railway

Newtonmore
1 km

River Spey

A9

Ruthven

Detail 'D'
250 m

Nuide Farm

Milton Burn

ruins

gate

Fernisdale 2

250

Milton of Nuide

ford

Detail 'C'

Continued Glen A9

deer gate

The bridge over Milton Burn

The bothy at Luibleathann

General Wade's bn.

Milton Burn

to Phones

Loch an Dabhaich

ruin

Tromie 2

Contd. Glen

Continued Glen 2

Loch Cuaich is part of the Hydro-electric scheme described on 'Glen Tromie 1' receiving extra water from the Tromie generating power at Cuaich Power station and sending its increased volume of water over the River Truim via aqueduct and pipeline into Loch Ericht. It is this aqueduct that provides one approach to Loch Cuaich, the alternative being from the A889 near Cuaich. The track that follows the aqueduct has been used to assist access to the grouse butts on the surrounding moors. Beyond the Loch Cuaich dam the man-made features are at last left behind and the loch-side track climbs up to the wild moorland area, and suddenly provides views north to Newtonmore and Kingussie. A new track continues north to Phones where a right turn (see Glen Fernisdale) leads to Ruthven and Kingussie. Total distances are:-

Dalwhinnie to Phones 14 km (9 m)
Dalwhinnie to Kingussie 22 km (14 m)

Dalwhinnie has a 'frontier' feel about it - as if still trying to make a success of its harsh environment. The distillery keeps the place going. To the west Loch Ericht beckons - but that's another story!

Continued Loch Cuaich 2

'thumb nail' sketch of the bridge opposite the garage which is the start of the 'aqueduct route' to Loch Cuaich.

31

Loch Cuaich 2

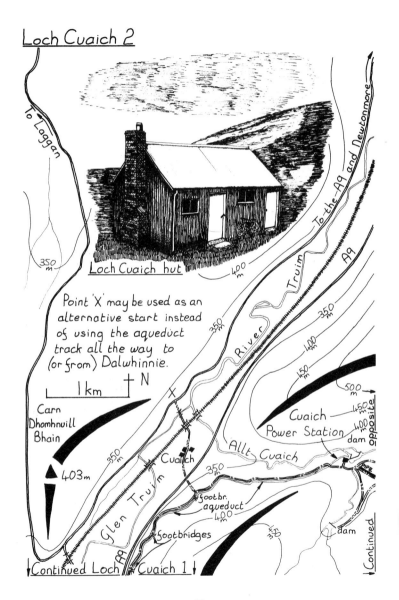

To Laggan

350 m

Loch Cuaich hut

To the A9 and Newtonmore

River Truim

400 m

A9

350 m

400 m

450 m

Point 'X' may be used as an alternative start instead of using the aqueduct track all the way to (or from) Dalwhinnie.

├── 1 km ──┤ ┼ N

350 m

X

500 m

Cuaich Power Station

450 m

400 m

dam

opposite

Carn Dhomhnuill Bhain

350 m

Cuaich

Allt Cuaich

350 m

▲ 403m

footbr. aqueduct

400 m

450 m

dam

Glen Truim

A9

footbridges

↓Continued Loch Cuaich 1↓

Continued→

32

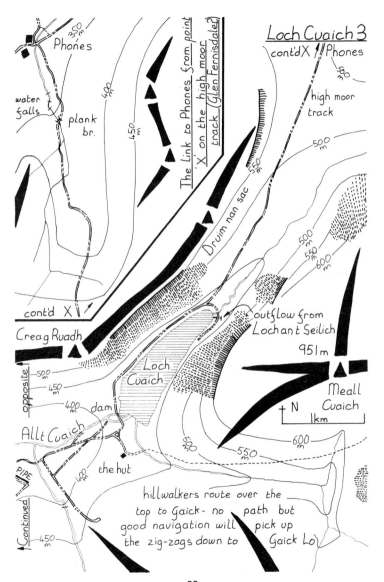

Phones

350 m

water
falls

plank
br.

400

450 m

The Link to Phones from point 'X' on the high moor track (Glen Fernisdale?)

Loch Cuaich 3

cont'd X   Phones

350

high moor
track

500

Druim nan sac

550

cont'd X →

Creag Ruadh

500

opposite

450 m

400

dam

Allt Cuaich

PIPE

Continued

450 m

400 m

the hut

Loch
Cuaich

outflow from
Loch an t Seilich

951 m

Meall
Cuaich

N   1km

500
550
600 m

500
550 m

550

600 m

hillwalkers route over the
top to Gaick - no path but
good navigation will pick up
the zig-zags down to Gaick Lo

33

Edendon Water 1

Edendon Water forms the southern half of the Gaick Pass which runs all the way from Dalnacardoch Lodge to the Tromie and Kingussie, the total distance being 41 km (25 m). The climb through Dalnacardoch wood soon gives way to open grouse moor and even though only minutes from the A9 one soon feels to be miles from anywhere. The track climbs little once out of the woods. There is a rough shed after 3km at Creag nan Sionnach and a bothy at Sronphadruig Lo, so shelter is never far away, but not so if the through route to Glen Tromie is planned. Refer to Glen Tromie as all is not 'plain sailing' even when past Loch an Duin due to a serious ford just south of Gaick Lodge. The path section from near the end of the 'Edendon Water' track along the side of Loch an Duin is not a bike ride. The walker's path is soft and wet, bikes must be carried or wheeled. Past the Loch the path crosses steep ground then fords the river before the track to Gaick is reached. _Note:_- cycling on the walkers path will bring mountainbiking into disrepute please don't spoil it for others!!

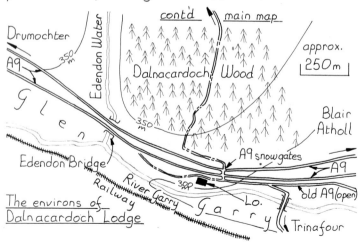

The environs of Dalnacardoch Lodge

34

<u>Sronphadruig Lodge</u>

Sronphadruig bothy is a
two-roomed cottage/outbuilding
100m behind the Lodge. A great
deal of work has been carried
out to make it a decent
shelter. Please look
after it!!

<u>Sronphadruig
Bothy</u>

to the Lodge
100m

Edendon Water 3

To the west of Edendon Water lies the vast area of the Dalnacardoch Forest. Totally wild – no tracks – nothing, until either the A9 is reached to the south and west or the Cuaich aqueduct to the north. Even the glens are over 400m (1200ft) high. Such an area is sacred and must remain untouched by bulldozer and "development". If, dear reader, you want to lose yourself this is just the place!

Sign at X :-
"Public footpath by Gaick Pass to Speyside". It does <u>not</u> say how far it is!

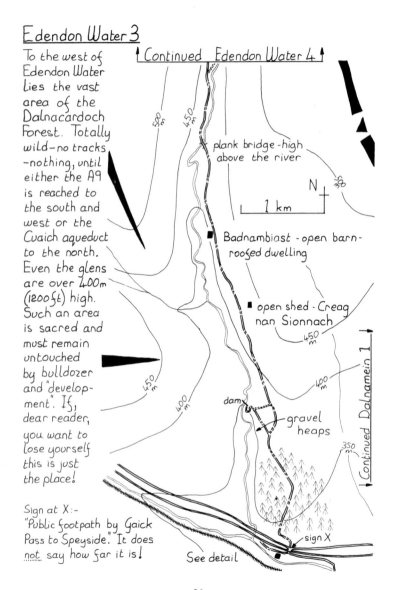

Continued Edendon Water 4

plank bridge - high above the river

N

1 km

Badnambiast - open barn - roofed dwelling

open shed - Creag nan Sionnach

dam

gravel heaps

Continued Dalnamein 1

sign X

See detail

36

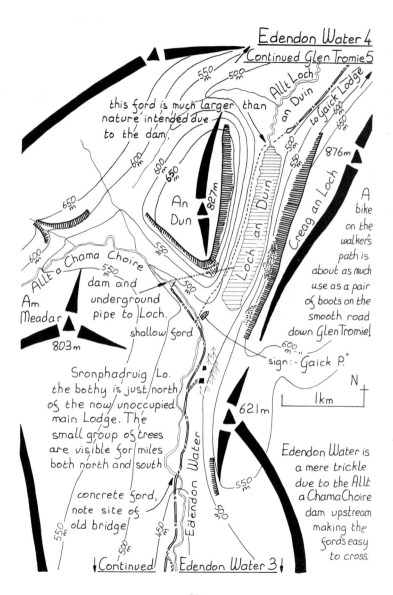

550 m
500 m

Allt Loch an Duin

to Gaick Lodge

this ford is much larger than nature intended due to the dam.

600 m

650 m

600 m
650 m

827 m

876 m

An Dun

650 m

600 m

Allt a Chama Choire

550 m

dam and underground pipe to Loch.

Am Meadar

803 m

shallow ford

500 m

Loch an Duin

Creag an Loch

A bike on the walkers path is about as much use as a pair of boots on the smooth road down Glen Tromie!

600 m

sign :- "Gaick P."

N

1 km

Sronphadruig Lo. the bothy is just north of the now unoccupied main Lodge. The small group of trees are visible for miles both north and south

621 m

Edendon Water

concrete ford, note site of old bridge

550 m

Edendon Water is a mere trickle due to the Allt a Chama Choire dam upstream making the fords easy to cross.

550 m

600 m

450 m

500 m

↓ Continued   Edendon Water 3 ↓

37

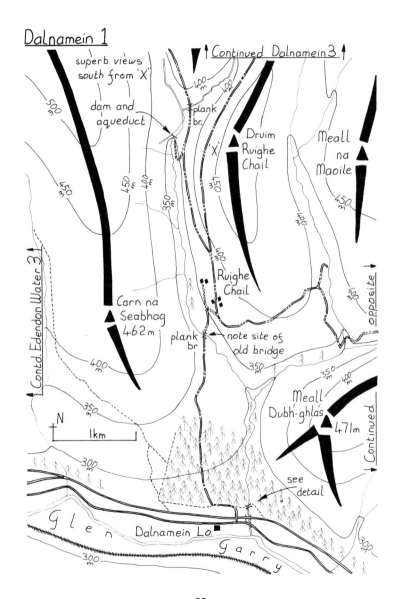

Dalnamein 1

superb views
south from 'X'

dam and
aqueduct

↑ Continued Dalnamein 3 ↑

plank
br.

Druim
Ruighe
Chail

'X'

Meall
na
Maoile

Contd. Edendon Water 3

Carn na
Seabhag
462m

Ruighe
Chail

plank
br. ← note site of
old bridge

opposite →

Meall
Dubh-ghlas
471m

Continued →

N

1km

see
detail

Glen Dalnamein Lo. Garry

500
m

450

450

400

350
m

400
m

450

400
m

400
m

400

350

350
m

400
m

300
m

350
m

400

350
m

300
m

300
m

300

The abandoned village of Ruighe Chail is one of the hidden gems of the "East of Drumochter" area. Countless thousands of people race up and down the A9, unaware, un-caring — but quietly tucked away above the woods lies a small piece of history. Here lies an insight into another age; a tough life farming in the high glens, with the ruins of the summer sheilings even higher up the glens.

Allt nam Ba

Allt a Chireachain

450 m

500 m

ford

bothy

450 m

opposite

400 m

dam

350 m

400 m

450 m

350 m

Continued Gleann a Chrombaidh 3

People lived, grew up and died in small settlements such as this in an age when the family meant everything and survival was a way of life. Our high-speed rat-race lifestyle — demonstrated so close by on the A9, contrasts so sharply with the simple life, with such basic values. But was it really so bad? Vandalism, mugging and graffiti were unknown; it was a "hard work - survive - help others" society instead of the present "leisure - greed - look - after - yourself" society. So much for progress! What a pity the old values are not combined with the progress of today, or perhaps that is impossible as "progress" itself brings out the worst in so many of us, and it is the availability of wealth and technology that makes some of us believe the old values no longer have a place. This is surely our biggest mistake! I digress, more on Dalnamein over.

Continued

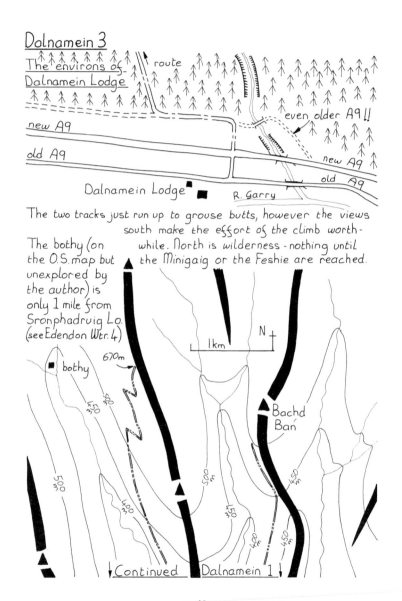

Dalnamein 3

The environs of Dalnamein Lodge

route

even older A9!!

new A9

old A9

new A9

old A9

Dalnamein Lodge

R. Garry

The two tracks just run up to grouse butts, however the views south make the effort of the climb worthwhile. North is wilderness - nothing until the Minigaig or the Feshie are reached.

The bothy (on the O.S. map but unexplored by the author) is only 1 mile from Sronphadruig Lo. (see Edendon Wtr. 4)

bothy

670m

1km

N

Bachd Ban

↓Continued   Dalnamein 1↓

40

Ruighe Chail:-
Portrait of a lost village

Some of
the ruins
of Ruighe
Chail

The A9
through
the ages
- three
bridges
at
Dalnamein

Gleann a Chrombaidh 1

The Gleann a Chrombaidh track leaps from one O.S. map to another in a most frustrating way so here it is in the middle of a page for a change! It provides a somewhat unremarkable route in to a glen, then rises to the upper reaches of the Dalnamein glens. By far the most interesting features of the route depicted are the bridges on General Wade's Military Road which may be visited by using the alternative start/finish points shown. There is an un-named bothy near the ford. The total distance from Clunes Lodge to the end of the track is 9km or 6 miles.

Tinkers Bridge

TINKERS BRIDGE

ALLT NAN CUINNEAG

The bothy.
The moor track crosses into the Dalnamein glen beyond.

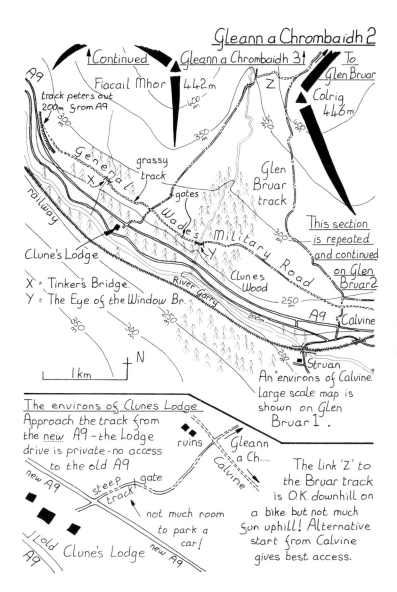

Gleann a Chrombaidh 2

↑Continued Gleann a Chrombaidh 3↑ To Glen Bruar

A9

Fiacail Mhor 442m

Colrig 446m

Z

track peters out 200m from A9

300m

350m

400m

350m

400m

General

grassy track

Glen Bruar track

350m

railway

gates

Wade's

Military Road

300m

This section is repeated and continued on Glen Bruar2

Clune's Lodge

X

Y

Clunes Wood

250m

X = Tinker's Bridge.
Y = The Eye of the Window Br.

River Garry

250m

200m

A9 Calvine

350m
300m

300m
350m

250m

200m

Struan

N
|—— 1 km ——|+

An 'environs of Calvine' large scale map is shown on Glen Bruar1.

The environs of Clunes Lodge

Approach the track from the **new** A9 – the Lodge drive is private - no access to the old A9

ruins

Gleann a Ch....
Calvine

new A9

steep track

gate

not much room to park a car!

old A9

Clune's Lodge

new A9

The link 'Z' to the Bruar track is O.K. downhill on a bike but not much fun uphill! Alternative start from Calvine gives best access.

43

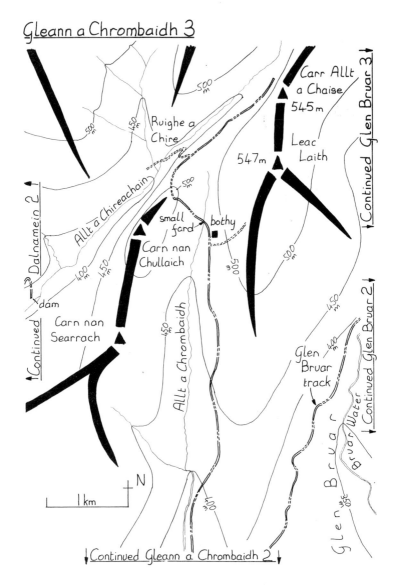

Carr Allt
a Chaise
545m

Leac
Laith

547m

Ruighe a
Chire

Allt a Chireachain

small
ford

bothy

Carn nan
Chullaich

Carn nan
Searrach

dam

Allt a Chrombaidh

Glen
Bruar
track

Glen Bruar

Bruar Water

N

1 km

↑ Dalnamein 2

↑ Continued

→ Continued Glen Bruar 3

→ Continued Glen Bruar 2

↓ Continued Gleann a Chrombaidh 2 ↓

Glen Bruar 1

Glen Bruar is a long glen ending abruptly at the foot of the walker's route over the Minigaig Pass. Alternative starting points to Calvine are either of the two routes out of Glen Banvie. The Falls of Bruar (NOT a bike ride) are well worth a visit and can be explored by footpath from Bruar (or via Baluain Wood from Blair Atholl). Bruar Lodge is a working sheep farm surely one of the most remote farms in the country. The track passes through the farm yard but please try to respect the privacy of the occupants of the Lodge, a lover of such a location may not welcome company! A table of distances from Calvine follows. Blair Atholl is about 2km or 1ml. further.

Junction with Banvie Burn track :- 6km (3½ miles)

Bruar Lodge (this is also the footpath link to the Glen Banvie/Glen Tilt link track):- 13km (8 miles)

Last bridge before Minigaig :- 18km (11 miles)

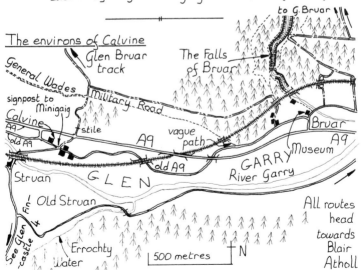

The environs of Calvine

to G. Bruar

Glen Bruar track

The Falls of Bruar

General Wades

Military Road

signpost to Minigaig

Calvine

A9

old A9

stile

vague path

A9

Bruar

A9

Museum

GARRY

River Garry

old A9

Struan

GLEN

Old Struan

See Glen Errochty

castle

Errochty Water

500 metres

N

All routes head towards Blair Atholl

45

Glen Bruar 2

↑Continued Glen Bruar 3↑

450m

400m

530m ▲

ford (not serious!)

▪ Ruichlachrie

450

350

B

r

u

a

r

350

Bruar Water

350

Ruichlachrie -unfortunately in a
state of near collapse but still
keeps the rain off – at least
it did May '91!!

↑Contd. Gleann a Chrombaidh 3↑

←Continued Gleann a Chrombaidh 2↑

←Continued Glen Banvie 2→

400m

350m

350

▲

Colrig
446m

400m

Best route
up Glen Bruar is
via Colrig returning
via the woods next
to Bruar Water.
The Falls
of Bruar

350m

G
l
e
n

Allt a Chrombaidh

300

N

1 km

300m

General Wade's
Military Road

A9

See detail
previous page

R. Garry

Calvine

A9

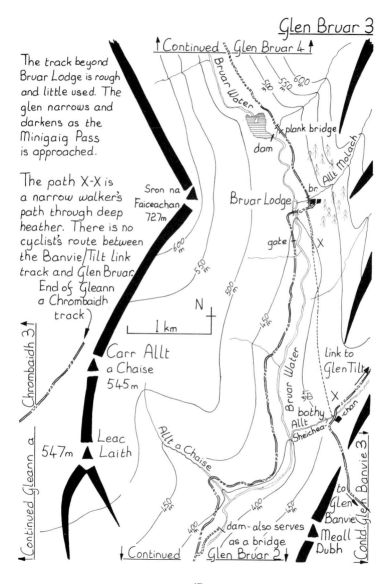

↑Continued Glen Bruar 4↑

Bruar Water

500 550 600
520 570

plank bridge

dam

Allt Molach

br.

The track beyond Bruar Lodge is rough and little used. The glen narrows and darkens as the Minigaig Pass is approached.

Sron na Faiceachan 727m

Bruar Lodge

The path X-X is a narrow walker's path through deep heather. There is no cyclist's route between the Banvie/Tilt link track and Glen Bruar.

gate

X

600m

550m

End of Gleann a Chrombaidh track

Chrombaidh 3↑

Carr Allt a Chaise 545m

500m

N

1 km

450m

Bruar Water

link to Glen Tilt

Leac Laith

547m

Allt a Chaise

350

X

bothy

Continued Gleann a↓

150m

Allt Sheichea

chan

Contd Glen Banvie 3↓

150m

400m

to Glen Banvie

150m

400m

dam - also serves as a bridge

↓Continued Glen Bruar 2↓

Meall Dubh

47

Glen Bruar 4

The head of Glen Bruar divides into a complex pattern of extremely remote steep sided glens. A mountainbike can be ridden up the rough track to the last bridge. Any further exploration must be on foot. The Minigaig Pass is a high level wild mountain walk eventually emerging on Glen Tromie 3 map. The central section of the Minigaig Pass is for experienced mountain walkers ONLY.

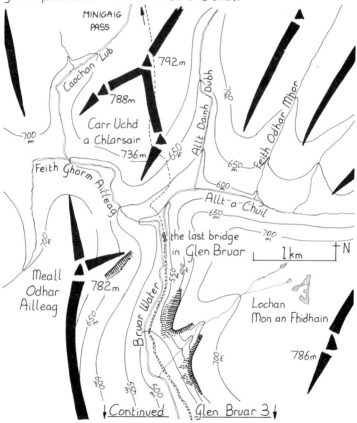

↓Continued   Glen Bruar 3↓

<u>Glen Bruar 5</u>

North of the map opposite must be one of the least frequented and remote areas in Scotland. The terrain is unremarkable save for its isolation. North lies the great watershed between the River Garry with its tributaries Bruar and Tilt and the River Spey with its tributaries Tromie and Feshie whilst north east the Geldie seeks out the Dee. Wilderness such as this must be protected - especially from the bull-dozer! The very tracks featured in these pages are enough - many are built without planning permission - it is surely time to call a halt however good these tracks are for the mountainbiker and long distance walker.

<u>Bruar Lodge</u>

<u>The last bridge in Glen Bruar</u>

Glen Banvie 1

Glen Banvie is, strictly, only a correct title for the section of track running from Blair Atholl to Glen Bruar but within this chapter the more northerly link to Bruar Lodge (a walker's route) and the new link track to Glen Tilt are included. Glen Banvie therefore provides two alternative starts to Glen Bruar and a superb round trip via the Tilt, and a "bike-assisted" start for walkers bound for Beinn Dearg. A bothy and a hut provide shelter if the weather breaks. Scenery from woodland to wild moor provides variety. Views down into Glen Bruar and up into the higher reaches of the Tilt whet the appetite for more. The starting points for Glen Banvie are complex so refer to "Glen Bruar 1" and "The environs of Blair Atholl" for clarification. The tracks in Balvain Wood provide short routes following the contours of the hillside between Bruar falls and the beautiful wooded ravine of the lower Banvie Burn.

Evening sunlight picks out the front of the bothy on the bank of Allt Sheicheachan

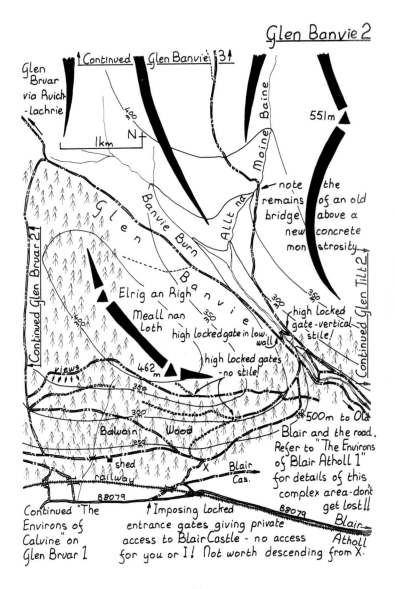

Glen Bruar via Ruich-lachrie

↑Continued Glen Banvie 3↑

Moine Baine

551m

1km N

Glen

Banvie Burn

Allt na

note the remains of an old bridge above a new concrete monstrosity→

Continued Glen Bruar 2↑

Glen Banvie

Elrig an Righ

Meall nan Loth

high locked gate in low wall

high locked gate -vertical stile!

Continued Glen Tilt 2↓

462m

high locked gates -no stile!

views↑↑↑

Balwain Wood

shed railway

X Blair Cas.

※500m to Old Blair and the road. Refer to "The Environs of Blair Atholl 1" for details of this complex area-don't get lost!!

B8079

Blair Atholl

B8079

Continued "The Environs of Calvine" on Glen Bruar 1

↑Imposing locked entrance gates giving private access to Blair Castle - no access for you or I ! Not worth descending from X.

Glen Banvie 3

The new track beyond Allt Sheicheachan Bothy is yet another blot on the landscape, however this links up with the track from Glen Tilt which used to end at the Allt Stanaidh hut, making an excellent round trip. The walker's path to Glen Bruar passes through deep heather and is not a route for even the most mountainous mountainbike!!

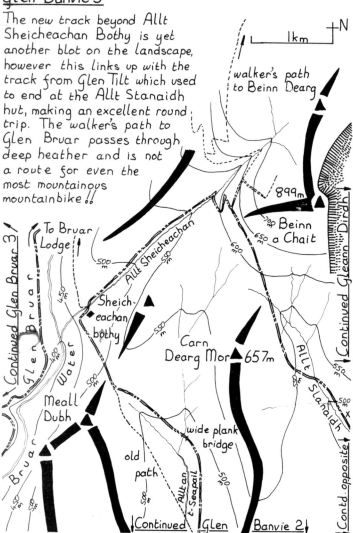

To Bruar Lodge

walker's path to Beinn Dearg

899m

Beinn a Chait

650m

Continued Gleann Dirdh

Allt Sheicheachan

500m

Sheicheachan bothy

Carn Dearg Mor ▲ 657m

600

Allt Stanaidh

550m

500m

X

Continued Glen Bruar 3

Glen Bruar Water

450m

400m

Meall Dubh

500m

wide plank bridge

old path

Bruar

450m

500m

Alltan t-Seapail

500m

Continued Glen Banvie 2

Contd opposite

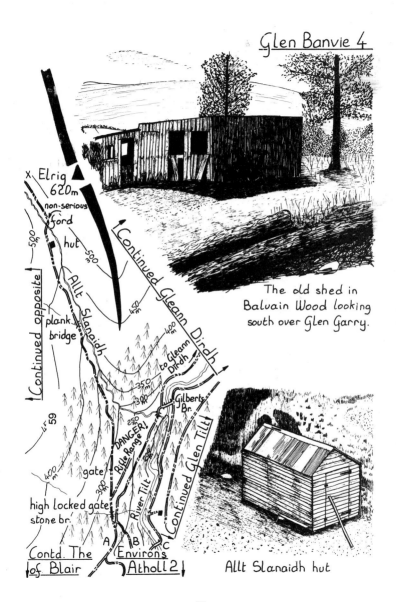

X Elrig
620m
non-serious
ford
hut

500
300

Continued Gleann Dirdh

Continued opposite

500
300

Allt Slanaidh

plank
bridge

400m

400
m

to Gleann
Dirdh

350
m
300

Gilberts
Br.

250
m

DANGER!
Rifle Range!

Continued Glen Tilt

gate

400
m

300

River Tilt

200m

high locked gate
stone br.

A B
C

Contd. The
of Blair

Environs
Atholl 2

The old shed in
Balvain Wood looking
south over Glen Garry.

Allt Slanaidh hut

Tilt to Cairnwell

Access:- Access to the routes in the Tilt to Cairnwell area is from three main points only. Blair Atholl leads to the Glen Tilt area and Glen Girnaig. The A924 Pitlochry-Bridge of Cally/ Blairgowrie road gives access to Glen Fearnach, Glen Loch and Enochdhu. The third point of access is Spittal of Glenshee for Glen Taitneach (and Lochsie). The loner is the Baddoch Burn, starting at the northern side of The Cairnwell on the way to Braemar. Only Blair Atholl boasts a railway station.

Accommodation:- Apart from expensive hotels the area is poorly served with accommodation. There are of course all facilities in Blair Atholl, including two camp sites. Also, south of Killiecrankie there is a good camp site at Faskally. Strath Ardle and Glenshee have little to offer: no youth hostels and sparse camping facilities, mostly closed in winter.

Geographical Features:- Apart from the environs of Blair Atholl the region comprises scattered farms at low level in the glens and mile upon mile of wild moorland and high mountain scenery. The routes in this section are for the lover of wild places; none of the routes offer much in the way of shelter and the intrepid explorer should have a high regard for the fitness, equipment and experience required. The rewards are long routes offering both a challenge and a feeling of solitude.

Mountains:- The west of the region is dominated by Beinn a Ghlo and Carn Laith with Ben Vrackie to the south west. The east of the region is watched over by Beinn Iutharn Mhor and Carn a Rhig with the skiers .Cairnwell to the side of the

56

A93. Fortunately the ski lifts and general shambles around the summit of the 'Devils Elbow' road to Braemar is not visible to the explorer of these glens.

Rivers:- As always rivers are major features of all long distance cross country routes and it is very difficult to describe the size of any particular ford. A study of the map and this book as well as weather/snowmelt conditions is essential before setting off. The size of a river can be judged by studying the extent of the area it drains. Baddoch Burn drains into the River Dee but all other rivers in this section end up in the Tay via either the Garry, Tummel, River Ardle or Shee Water and Black Water.

Forests:- Not many! Not even as many as the O.S. maps depict! (see Glen Lochsie). The woods of Blair Atholl are referred to earlier and apart from a few small plantations there are sadly no other forests.

Lochs:- Loch Loch is the star of the area, in a grand setting overshadowed by Beinn a Ghlo. Note this drains north, Glen Loch is double-ended. Loch Moraig is a pleasant sheet of water passed up Glen Fender and Loch nan Eun at the head of Gleann Taitneach is the crossing point for many walker's routes and a starting point for the ascent of several fine mountains. I must admit not investigating the wild Loch Vrotachan between The Cairnwell and Baddoch Burn. Finally Loch Crannoch lies to the east of Gleann Fearnach.

Emergency:- If away from the roadside in this area you are very much on your own. Forest Lodge in Glen Tilt, Shinagag in Glen Girnaig, Daldhu and Feolar Lo. in Gleann Fearnach are occupied. Baddoch Burn starts at a 'phone box, another is 2km S.W. of Spittal of Glenshee (os ref: 126686) and another at Kirkmichael 3km south of Enochdhu or 5km south of Bridgend, Gleann Fearnach.

Tilt to Cairnwell Routes 1

Glen Tilt

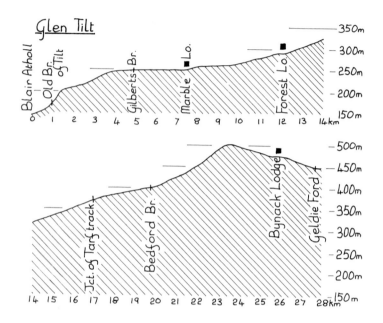

Gleann Diridh and Gleann Mhairc

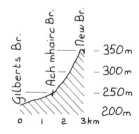

58

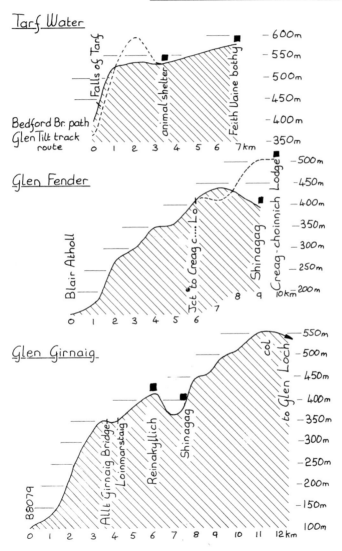

Tarf Water

Bedford Br. path
Glen Tilt track
route

Falls of Tarf
animal shelter
Feith Uaine bothy

- 600m
- 550m
- 500m
- 450m
- 400m
- 350m

0 1 2 3 4 5 6 7km

Glen Fender

Blair Atholl
Jct to Creag c.... Loch
Shinagag
Creag-choinnich Lodge

- 500m
- 450m
- 400m
- 350m
- 300m
- 250m
- 200m

0 1 2 3 4 5 6 7 8 9 10km

Glen Girnaig

B8079
Allt Girnaig Bridge
Loinmarstaig
Reinakyllich
Shinagag
col to Glen Loch

- 550m
- 500m
- 450m
- 400m
- 350m
- 300m
- 250m
- 200m
- 150m
- 100m

0 1 2 3 4 5 6 7 8 9 10 11 12km

59

Tilt to Cairnwell Routes 3

Gleann Fearnach

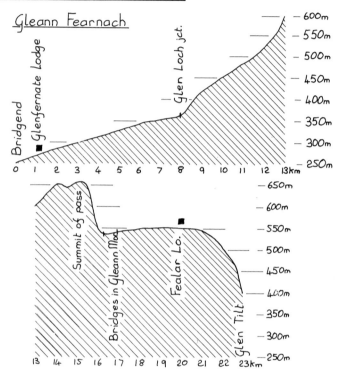

Glen Loch

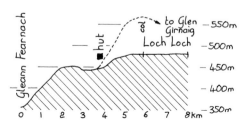

Enochdhu

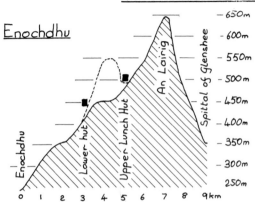

Gleann Taitneach

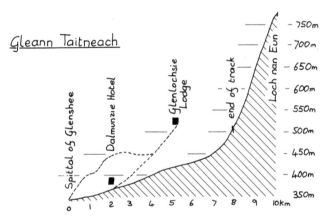

Baddoch Burn

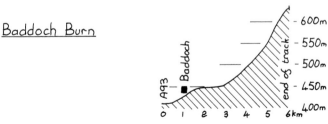

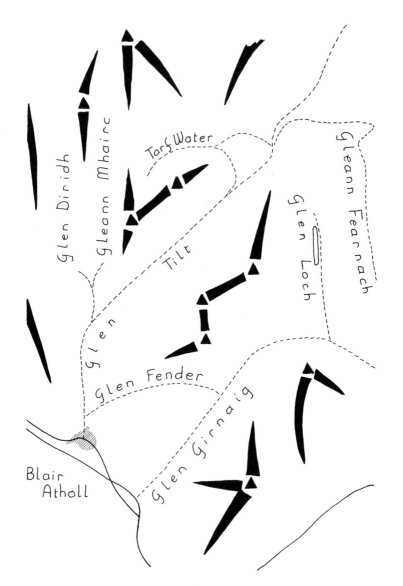

Glen Diridh

Gleann Mhairc

Tarf Water

Gleann Fearnach

Glen Loch

Tilt

Glen

Glen Fender

Glen Girnaig

Blair Atholl

62

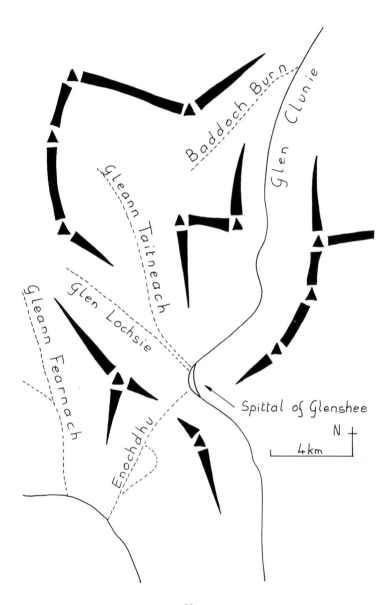

Baddoch Burn

Glen Clunie

Gleann Taitneach

Glen Lochsie

Gleann Fearnach

Enochdhu

Spittal of Glenshee

N

4 km

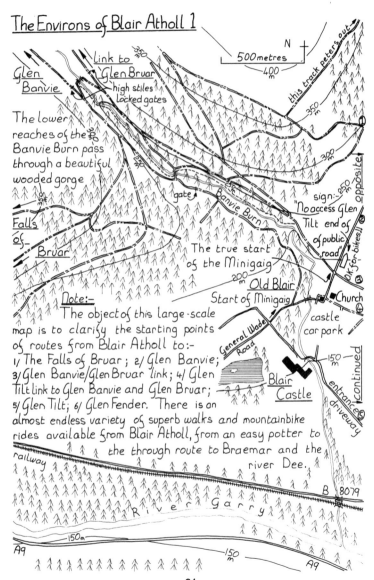

The Environs of Blair Atholl 1

N

500 metres

400 m

this track peters out

Glen Banvie

Link to Glen Bruar

high stiles locked gates

350 m

350 m

300 m

250 m

The lower reaches of the Banvie Burn pass through a beautiful wooded gorge

Falls of Bruar

gate

Banvie Burn

sign:- "No access Glen Tilt end of of public road"

opposite

bk. for bikes!!

The true start of the Minigaig

200 m

Old Blair

Start of Minigaig

Church

castle car park

Note:-
The object of this large-scale map is to clarify the starting points of routes from Blair Atholl to:-
1/ The Falls of Bruar; 2/ Glen Banvie;
3/ Glen Banvie/Glen Bruar link; 4/ Glen Tilt link to Glen Banvie and Glen Bruar;
5/ Glen Tilt; 6/ Glen Fender. There is an almost endless variety of superb walks and mountainbike rides available from Blair Atholl, from an easy potter to the through route to Braemar and the river Dee.

General Wade Road

Blair Castle

150 m

entrance driveway

continued

railway

B 8079

River Garry

150 m

A9

150 m

A9

64

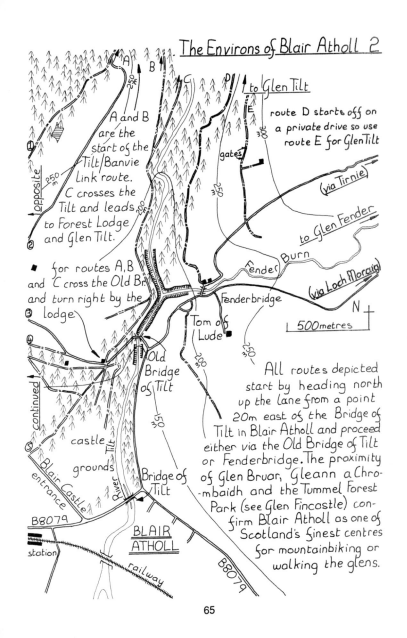

The Environs of Blair Atholl 2

(A) (B)
C
D
to Glen Tilt

250
E

A and B
are the
start of the
Tilt/Banvie
Link route.
C crosses the
Tilt and leads
to Forest Lodge
and Glen Tilt.

route D starts off on
a private drive so use
route E for Glen Tilt

300

opposite

250 m

gates

200

250

(1)

(2)

• for routes A,B
and C cross the Old Br.
and turn right by the
(3) lodge

350

(via Tirnie)

to Glen Fender

Fender Burn

(via Loch Moraig)

Fenderbridge

(4)

200

Tom of
Lude

N

500 metres

Old
Bridge
of Tilt

250

200
300

350

continued

(5)

castle
grounds

Blair Castle
entrance

River Tilt

Bridge of
Tilt

All routes depicted
start by heading north
up the lane from a point
20m east of the Bridge of
Tilt in Blair Atholl and proceed
either via the Old Bridge of Tilt
or Fenderbridge. The proximity
of Glen Bruar, Gleann a Chro-
-mbaidh and the Tummel Forest
Park (see Glen Fincastle) con-
firm Blair Atholl as one of
Scotland's finest centres
for mountainbiking or
walking the glens.

B8079

station

railway

BLAIR
ATHOLL

B8079

Glen Tilt 1

Glen Tilt is said by many to be the most beautiful glen in all Scotland. I have yet to hear this statement challenged. Personally I have looked forward with anticipation for three years to exploring Glen Tilt, ever since looking across the Geldie Burn above Glen Dee whilst researching 'The Cairngorm Glens'. I was not disappointed, Glen Tilt has beautiful woods and raging rivers in its lower reaches. The glen turns as if hiding its charms then runs straight as an arrow to the magnificent Falls of Tarf before another straight narrow section gives way to the open strath forming the watershed dividing the Tilt from the Geldie. Here is a major ford, the piers of the old bridge standing 100m upstream. Some believe this bridge should be replaced but limited access maintains the remote nature of the area. Through routes are only for dry weather. Glen Tilt is long and a bike may be used by walkers to gain access to the upper reaches. Through routes exist (via the ford) to Linn of Dee and Braemar and to Feshiebridge via the Geldie/Feshie Link. These routes are very long and committing. Blair Atholl to Feshiebridge is one of the longest cross country routes in Scotland. A table of distances follows:—

from Blair Atholl to:-

Gilberts Bridge	5km	3 m
Forest Lodge	12km	7.5m
Tarf track jct	17km	10.5m
Bedford Bridge	20km	12.5m
Bynack Lodge	26km	16 m
Geldie Ford	27.5km	17m

There is NO SHELTER in Glen Tilt

IF the Geldie Burn can be safely crossed the options for long through routes are given below. Full details are given in Book 1 "The Cairngorm Glens".

Either:-			Or:-		
Geldie Lodge	33km	20.5m	White Bridge	30km	19m
Eidart Bridge	38km	23.5m	Linn of Dee	35km	22 m
Feshiebridge	60km!	37 m	Braemar	45km	28 m

66

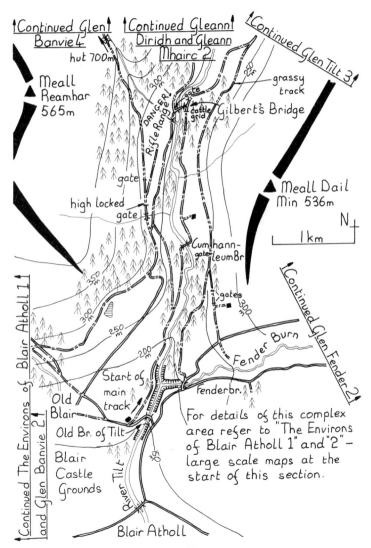

Continued Glen Banvie 4
hut 700m

Meall Reamhar 565m

Continued Gleann Diridh and Gleann Mhairc 2

Continued Glen Tilt 3

DANGER. Rifle Range.
gate
cattle grid
Gilbert's Bridge
grassy track

gate

high locked gate

Meall Dail Min 536m

N

1km

Cumhann-gate leum Br.

gates

Fender Burn

Continued Glen Fender 2

Start of main track

fenderbr.

Old Blair

Old Br. of Tilt

Blair Castle Grounds

River Tilt

For details of this complex area refer to "The Environs of Blair Atholl 1" and "2" – large scale maps at the start of this section.

Continued The Environs of Blair Atholl 1
Continued The Environs of Blair Atholl 2 and Glen Banvie 2

Blair Atholl

Marble Lodge
and
Gaw's Bridge

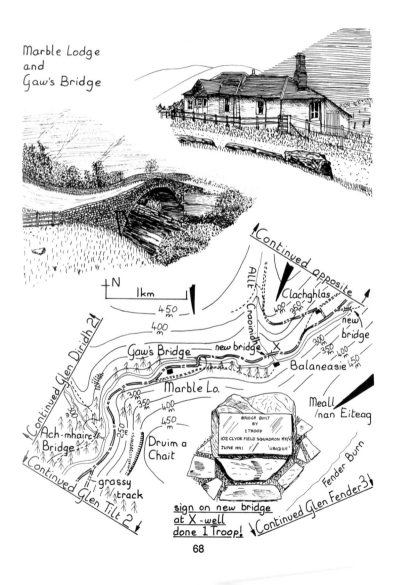

↑N |—— 1km ——|

450 m

400 m

Continued Glen Diridh 2↑

Allt Craoinidh

Continued opposite↗

Clachghlas

400m 350m

new bridge

300m 350m 400m 450m

Gaw's Bridge

new bridge

X

Balaneasie

Marble Lo.

300m 350m 400m 450m

Continued Glen Tilt 2↑

Ach-mhairc Bridge

25E

Druim a Chait

grassy track

Meall nan Eiteag

Fender Burn

Continued Glen Fender 3↓

BRIDGE BUILT
BY
1 TROOP
102 CLYDE FIELD SQUADRON REV
JUNE 1991   'UBIQUE'

sign on new bridge
at X - well
done 1 Troop!

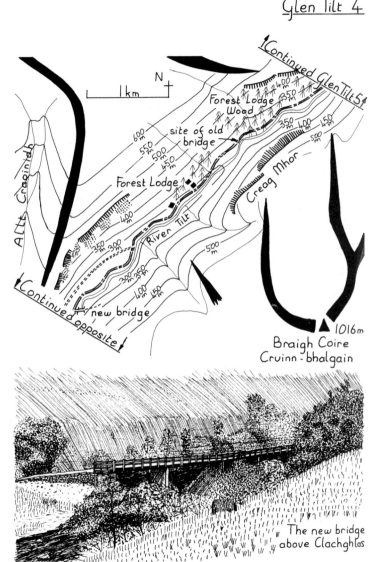

Continued Glen Tilt 5

Forest Lodge Wood

site of old bridge

Forest Lodge

Allt Craoinidh

River Tilt

Creag Mhor

Continued opposite

new bridge

1016m
Braigh Coire
Cruinn-bhalgain

The new bridge
above Clachghlas

Glen Tilt 5

The Falls of
Tarf from
Bedford Bridge

THIS BRIDGE WAS ERECTED IN 1886
WITH FUNDS CONTRIBUTED BY
HIS FRIENDS AND OTHERS AND BY
THE SCOTTISH RIGHTS OF WAY SOCIETY LTD
TO COMMEMORATE THE DEATH OF
FRANCIS JOHN BEDFORD, AGED 18
WHO WAS DROWNED NEAR HERE
ON 25TH AUGUST 1879

Continued Tarf Water?

Tarf Water

Continued opposite

new track

N

786 m   1 km

835 m

An Lochain (drains Loch Loch)

550 m   500 m   450 m   400 m

Tilt

Creag a Chrochaidh

450 m   400 m   350 m   400 m   450 m

River   550 m

350 m   500 m

Continued Glen Tilt 4

550 m

898 m
Meall a
Mhuirich

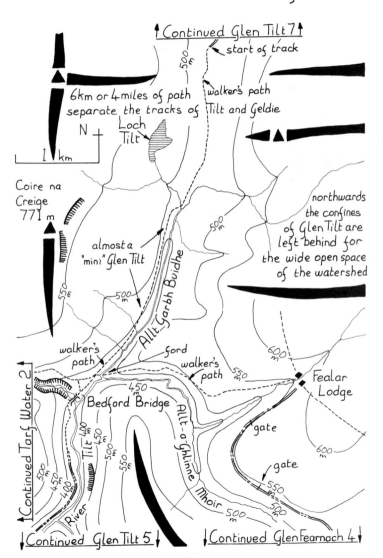

Continued Glen Tilt 7

start of track

walker's path

6km or 4 miles of path separate the tracks of Tilt and Geldie

N

1 km

Loch Tilt

Coire na Creige 771 m

almost a "mini" Glen Tilt

Allt Garbh Buidhe

northwards the confines of Glen Tilt are left behind for the wide open space of the watershed

walker's path

ford

walker's path

Fealar Lodge

Bedford Bridge

gate

gate

Allt a Ghlinne Mhoir

River Tilt

Continued Tarf Water 2

Continued Glen Tilt 5

Continued Glen Fearnach 4

71

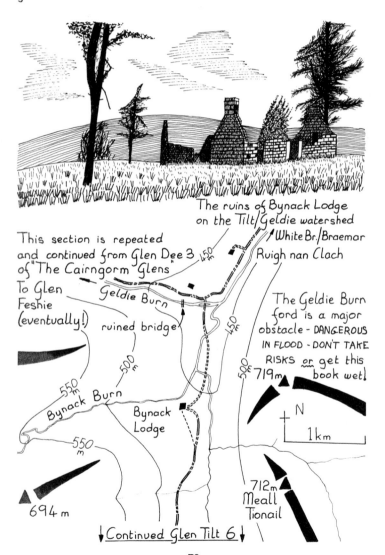

The ruins of Bynack Lodge
on the Tilt/Geldie watershed

White Br./Braemar

This section is repeated
and continued from Glen Dee 3
of "The Cairngorm Glens"

Ruigh nan Clach

To Glen
Feshie
(eventually!)

Geldie Burn

450 m

ruined bridge

The Geldie Burn
ford is a major
obstacle - DANGEROUS
IN FLOOD - DON'T TAKE
RISKS or get this
book wet!

450 m

500 m

550 m

500 m

719 m

Bynack Burn

Bynack
Lodge

N

1 km

550 m

694 m

712 m
Meall
Tionail

↓ Continued Glen Tilt 6 ↓

Glen Tilt 8

Bedford Bridge crosses the deep
pool at the foot of the Falls of Tarf
-crossing would otherwise be impossible
as Francis John Bedford discovered at
the ultimate cost - his life.

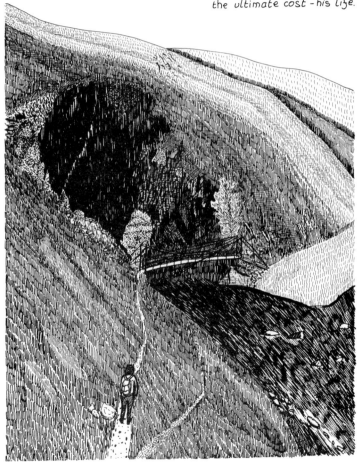

Gleann Diridh and Gleann Mhairc 1

Gleann Diridh and Gleann Mhairc are included not as long routes but as a short side-trip from Glen Tilt – a unique opportunity to view so easily two extremely remote glens, almost completely untouched by man. These are walkers glens although a bike may be used for the approach. The rivers join and through a series of rapids and falls drain into the Tilt. The starting point is about a mile below the confluence with the Tilt at Gilbert's Bridge. A confusing array of deer fencing needs to be avoided by keeping to the grassy slopes above. Your hard working author descended too far below Ach mhairc Bridge and had to struggle back up to circumnavigate the fencing – there is <u>no</u> way out ! The two bridges are the only man made features (apart from the fence) the rest is pure wilderness.

The Environs of Gilberts Bridge

Gleann Diridh and Gleann Mhairc

Glen Tilt

River Tilt

50m

N

cattle grid

gate

sign warning of rifle range to the south

Gilberts Br.

Blair Atholl

rifle range

<u>Ach mhairc Bridge</u>
- almost hidden in the dense woodland - don't fall in !

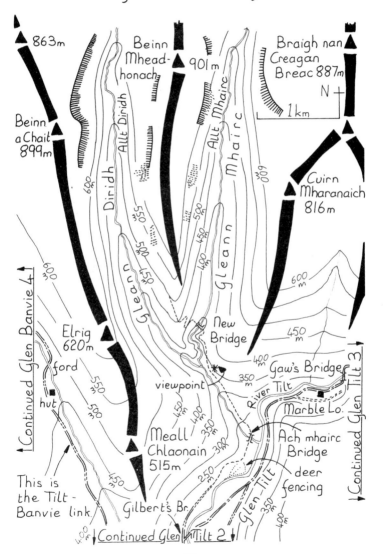

863m

Beinn
Mheadhonach
901m

Braigh nan
Creagan
Breac 887m

N

1 km

Beinn
a Chait
899m

Alt Diridh

Alt Mhairc

Cuirn
Mharanaich
816m

Diridh

Gleann

Gleann Mhairc

600
m

600

← Continued Glen Banvie 4

600
m

Elrig
620m

New
Bridge

450
m

600
m

ford

hut

viewpoint

Gaw's Bridge

River Tilt

350
m

400
m

Marble Lo.

Continued Glen Tilt 3 →

Ach mhairc
Bridge

Meall
Chlaonain
515m

Glen Tilt

deer
fencing

Continued Glen Tilt 2 →

This is
the Tilt-
Banvie link

Gilbert's Br.

← Continued Glen Tilt 2 →

Tarf Water 1

Exploring the Tarf is no 'doddle'. Merely getting to the start of the Tarf track involves a 17km/11m trip up Glen Tilt from Blair Atholl or 20km/12.5m to Bedford Bridge, and that is only the start. The Tarf bothy is not maintained other than sporadic attention from Glasgow C.T.C. Affectionately known as the Tarf Hotel due to an old AA sign on the door. The track ends at an animal shelter and a particularly hair-raising bridge consisting of only two strands of wire. Wading the Tarf is safer if it is not in flood. If it is in flood the best advice is not to use the bridge either!

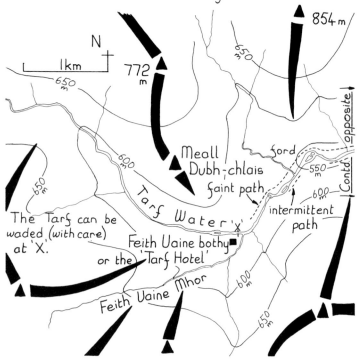

N

1km

854m

772 m

650
m

650
m

650
m

600
m

650
m

Meall
Dubh-chlais

faint path

ford

550
m

600
m

Contd. opposite

Tarf Water 'X'

intermittent
path

The Tarf can be
waded (with care)
at 'X'.

Feith Uaine bothy
or the 'Tarf Hotel'

Feith Uaine Mhor

600
m

650
m

The path from the animal shelter to Bedford Bridge
is very rough - slow going for the most experienced
walker. To appreciate this area fully one or two
nights out are needed - only then can the remote
reaches of the Tarf be fully appreciated. From the
'Hotel' pathless routes to Glen Bruar, Gleann Mhairc
the Geldie Burn and Glen Feshie are possible for the
experienced and fit. The entire area is a very
serious proposition in winter. Bedford Bridge to the
'Hotel' is 7km or 4·5 miles, distance from
the Tarf track
is about the
same.

882m

799m

771m

Coire na Creige

650m

N

1km

600m

550m

dodgy two-wire bridge!

faint path

very rough path

500m

Tarf Water

intermittent path

animal shelter

600m

Dun Mor

692m

Falls of Tarf

Bedford Br.

600m

450m

400m

new track - a mess, not included on principle !!

An Sligearnach
786m

600m

550m

500m

450m

400m

Glen Tilt

R. Tilt

Continued opposite

Continued

Glen Tilt 6

Continued

Glen Tilt 5

Tarf Water 3

<u>Feith Uaine Bothy</u>
— known as
the "Tarf Hotel"
complete with
old AA sign and
the remains of
a central heating
system — alas no
longer working!

The wire rope bridge over the Tarf makes
wading seem a very attractive option!

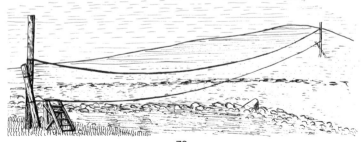

Yet another route starting in Blair Atholl, Glen Fender's metalled road passes one of the starting points for Glen Tilt and rises steeply to Loch Moraig. The road is unfenced and passes through cattle fields so if you don't like bulls — tough! The one your author encountered seemed contented enough with his harem of cows and totally disinterested in mountainbikers. I digress! The track to Monzie looks a bit private so to avoid the intrusion the route via the two sheds is recommended. The section from the huts to Creag-choinnich Lodge is rough — as are parts of the link into Glen Girnaig - see the next chapter. A further walker's link via Glen Loch to Gleann Fearnach is feasible or back to the Tilt (which has to be forded!). Study the relevant sections - these are long routes for the experienced walker or wilderness cyclist. However, Glen Fender alone or combined with Glen Girnaig makes a worthwhile outing.

The remains of Creag-chonnich Lodge.

Glen Fender 2

The environs of the sheep wash (see opposite)

Note X :- When returning from Creag-coinnich Lodge keep left near the fence and wall - the right hand (main) track is not the way.

Note the proximity of Marble Lodge in Glen Tilt (to the same scale).

200m

N

Creag-choinnich Lodge

this is the track to use

wall

gate

brick shed

sheep wash

wall

wall

Monzie

gap

gate

fence

wall

Note 'X'

the huts

↑Continued Glen Tilt 3↑

N

1km

450 m

450 m

400 m

Fender Burn

400 m

400 m

↑Continued Glen Tilt 2↑

350 m

300 m

Tirnie

Monzie

200 m

Fender Burn

300 m

Old Br of Tilt

preferred route

X

Loch Moraig

Contd opposite

R. Tilt

50

Blair Atholl

For details of this complex area refer to "The Environs of Blair Atholl 1" and "2" - large scale maps at the start of this section. The route follows the arrow at X through a gate.

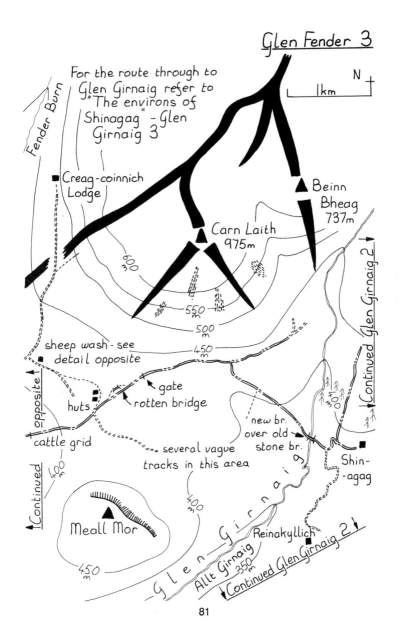

Glen Fender 3

N
|— 1km —|

For the route through to
Glen Girnaig refer to
"The environs of
Shinagag" - Glen
Girnaig 3

Fender Burn

Creag-coinnich
Lodge

Beinn
Bheag
737m

Carn Laith
975m

600
m

550
m

500
m

450
m

sheep wash - see
detail opposite

opposite ↑

huts

gate
rotten bridge

new br.
over old
stone br.

Shin-
agag

cattle grid

400
m

several vague
tracks in this area

400
m

← Continued Glen Girnaig 2

Continued Glen Girnaig 2 →

Meall Mor

450
m

Glen Girnaig

Reinakyllich

Allt Girnaig

350
m

Continued Glen Girnaig 2 ↓

Glen Girnaig 1

Glen Girnaig is slow going uphill as the upper reaches are rough from the Allt Girnaig crossing to Shinagag (and beyond if Loch Loch is the objective) The main access to Shinagag is via Glen Fender. Either Glen Girnaig or Glen Fender may be used as the start of the link route to Loch Loch and Glen Fearnach. There is shelter at Loinmarstaig. The distance from Killiecrankie to Shinagag is 11km or about 7 miles.

The start of the route leads under the A9

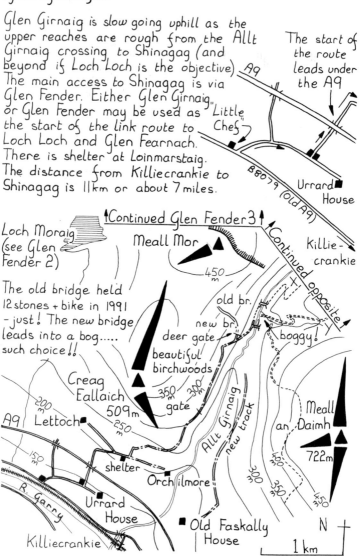

A9

"Little" Chef

B8079 (old A9)

Urrard House

↑Continued Glen Fender 3↑

Loch Moraig (see Glen Fender 2)

Meall Mor

Continued opposite

Killie-crankie

450 m

The old bridge held 12 stones + bike in 1991 - just! The new bridge leads into a bog..... such choice!!

old br.

new br.

deer gate

boggy!

beautiful birchwoods

Creag Eallaich 509m

350 m   300 m

gate

Allt Girnaig

new track

Meall an Daimh

722m

200 m

A9   Lettoch

250 m

150 m

shelter

Orchilmore

R. Garry

Urrard House

Old Faskally House

Killiecrankie

400   300   350   450   350   300

N

1 km

82

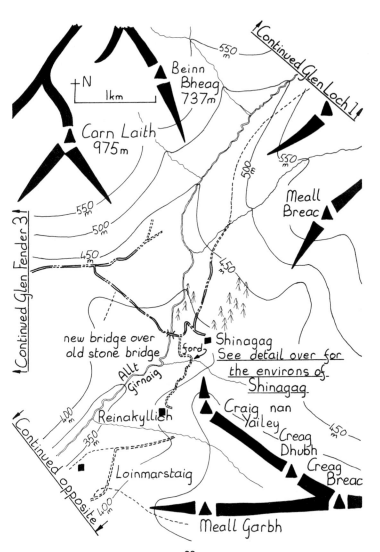

Continued Glen Loch 1

Beinn
Bheag
737m

550
m

N
1km

Carn Laith
975m

550
m

500
m

450
m

Continued Glen Fender 3

Meall
Breac

500
m

550
m

Shinagag
See detail over for
the environs of
Shinagag.

new bridge over
old stone bridge

ford

Allt
Girnaig

400
m

Reinakyllich

350
m

Continued opposite

Craig nan
Yailey

Creag
Dhubh

Creag
Breac

450

Loinmarstaig

400
m

Meall Garbh

83

Glen Girnaig 3

The environs of Shinagag

As Shinagag is approached from Glen Fender, Glen Girnaig can be seen to the right (south west). However, after a confusing area of twists and turns in the rather vague tracks near Shinagag the route then climbs to Reinakyllich and crosses 300m of pathless grass before joining the Glen Girnaig track to Loinmarstaig. Heading up Glen Girnaig go due north when the track meets the wall at 'X'

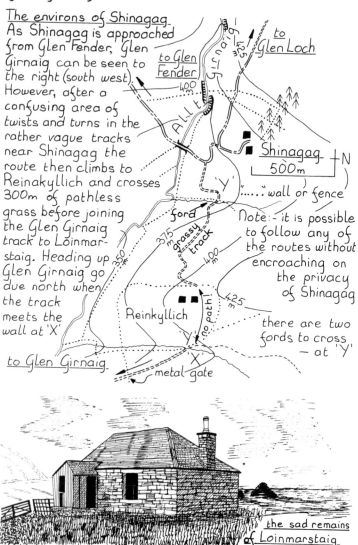

to Glen Fender

to Glen Loch

Allt Girnaig

400

425

Shinagag
500m

N

"wall or fence

ford

grassy track

375m

350

400m

Y

Note:- it is possible to follow any of the routes without encroaching on the privacy of Shinagag

there are two fords to cross — at 'Y'

Reinkyllich

no path!

425m

X

to Glen Girnaig

metal gate

the sad remains of Loinmarstaig

Gleann Fearnach 1

The trip up Gleann Fearnach starts from about a mile northwest of Enochdhu and continues up a metalled road as far as the junction with the Glen Loch track. The glen then narrows and steepens over the high pass into Gleann Mor and on to Fealar Lodge. The Lodge and its cottages are encountered with surprise:- an oasis of green grass in a wilderness of endless heather clad hills. The Lodge is a working sheep farm and its environs should be treated with respect especially during lambing. There is no shelter in the glen (though on the author's sorties the only shelter needed was from the blazing sun!). One must always be aware of the fact that the retreat from Fealar Lodge involves a considerable ascent over the pass. Long through routes to Glen Dee via White Bridge, and even the Spey via Glen Feshie are possible but these are very committing routes for the fit and experienced. The routes out of the head of Gleann Mor to the Tilt are not in the author's opinion a bike ride (but I know there are those of you who will ride almost anywhere! -please be careful not to offend walkers, farmers or sheep!).

A table of distances follows:- (from the A924)

Creag Liosk br.	5 km	3m
Daldhu (for Glen Loch)	8 km	5m
Summit of pass	13·5km	8·5m
Allt a Gh... B... waterfall	17km	11m
Fealar Lodge	20km	12·5m
Bedford Br. (Glen Tilt)	23km	14·5m
Geldie Burn (see G.Tilt 7)	30·5 km	19 m
Feshiebridge	63 km!	40m
Braemar	48 km	30 m

Refer to Glen Tilt 1 to compare distances. An alternative would be to return via the Tilt. Long routes for the connoisseur of distance wilderness exploration.

Gleann Fearnach 2

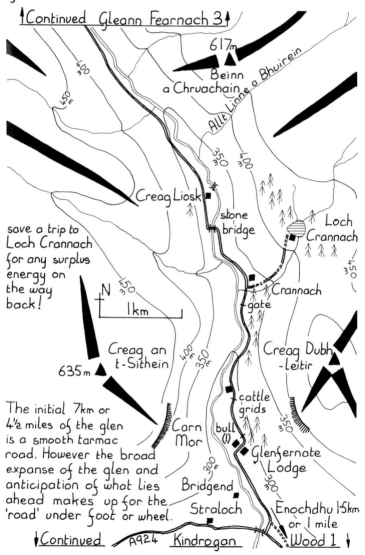

↑Continued Gleann Fearnach 3↑

617m

Beinn
a Chruachain

Allt Linne a Bhuirein

400
450m

350m
400m

Creag Liosk

stone
bridge

Loch
Crannach

save a trip to
Loch Crannach
for any surplus
energy on
the way
back!

450m

N

1km

Crannach

gate

Creag an
t-Sithein

635m▲

400m
350m

Creag Dubh
-Leitir

350m

The initial 7km or
4½ miles of the glen
is a smooth tarmac
road. However the broad
expanse of the glen and
anticipation of what lies
ahead makes up for the
'road' under foot or wheel.

Carn
Mor

cattle
grids

bull
(!)

Glenfernate
Lodge

300m

Bridgend

Straloch

300m

Enochdhu 1·5km
or 1 mile

↓Continued A924 Kindrogan Wood 1↓

↑ Continued Gleann Fearnach 4 ↑

Above Daldhu the glen narrows and the now unmade track steepens as it approaches the pass under Carn an t-Sionnaich. Once over the pass Gleann Mor awaits, Allt a Ghlinne Mhoir, its river, flows north to the Tilt. Past the col the intrepid explorer enters a truly remote glen connected only by this 655m pass (2150 ft) to the rest of civilisation - other than a footpath to upper Glen Tilt.

650m

gate

718m

Carn an t-Sionnaich
815m
858m

Carn Dallaig

ruins

722m

726m

669m
Sron Chrion a Bhacain

Allt Fearnach

to Glen Lochsie

650
600
550
500

↖ Continued Glen Loch 2 ↗

500m
450m

gate

400m

500
450

N

1km

400m
450m
500

Daldhu

Ben Vuirich
903m

↓ Cont'd Gleann Fearnach 2 ↓

Gleann Fearnach 4

↑Continued Glen Tilt 6↑

Fealar Lodge lies at the hub of routes from Strathardle to the Dee and Braemar, from Glen Tilt to Glen Shee. A wilderness crossing of some classic long distance routes.

550 m

500 m

Allt Garbh Buidhe

ford

Fealar Lodge

Tarf Water 2↑

Bedford Bridge

600 m

walkers

upper Gleann Mor

path to

gate

Allt a Ghlinne Bhig

↑Contd→

gate

550 m

Allt a Ghlinne

note the superb waterfall below the bridge

Continued Gleann Taitneach 2→

550 m

Allt a Ghlinne Mhoir

650 m

↓Continued Glen Tilt 5↓

Meall na Spionaig

1km   ↑N

650 m

Gleann Mor

650 m

650 m

↑Continued Gleann Fearnach 3↓

Fealar Lodge and the bridge near Creag Liosk

Glen Loch 1

Glen Loch is an easily accessible yet remote glen, the rough track into the glen extending only a couple of miles from the metalled road in Gleann Fearnach.

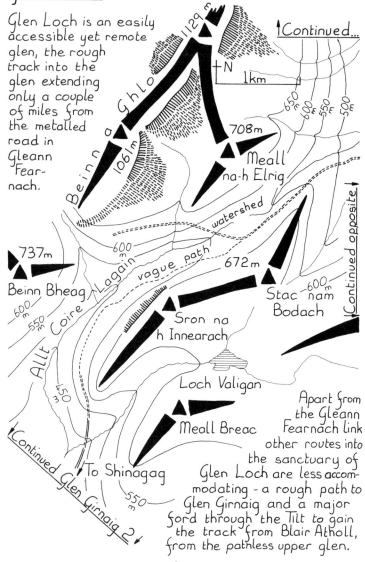

↑Continued...

N
1km

1129m

Beinn a Ghlo

1061m

708m

Meall na-h Elrig

watershed

600m

vague path

737m

Beinn Bheag

600m
550m

Allt Coire Lagain

672m

Stac nam Bodach
600m

Sron na h Innearach

Continued opposite →

Loch Valigan

450m

Meall Breac

550m

To Shinagag

←Continued Glen Girnaig 2 ↓

Apart from the Gleann Fearnach link other routes into the sanctuary of Glen Loch are less accommodating - a rough path to Glen Girnaig and a major ford through the Tilt to gain the track from Blair Atholl, from the pathless upper glen.

90

The start of the Glen Loch track from Daldhu is grassy but this soon becomes a rough, stony track. The fishing hut is properly called Bothan Ruigh-chuilein.

... Glen Loch 3 ↑

Sron Chrion a Bhacain
669 m

500 m
550 m

fishing hut

Allt Glen Loch

↑ Cont'd Gleann Fearnach 3 ↑

gate

500 m
550 m
600 m
650 m

450 m

400 m

Daldhu

↓ Cont'd Gleann Fearnach 2 ↓

← Continued opposite ↑

+N 1km

Ben Vurlich
903 m

Carn Dubh
868 m

The fishing hut is referred to as such due to the proximity of an upturned boat rather than the proximity of a loch!

The wild environs of Glen Loch are dominated by Beinn a Ghlo and Ben Vurlich.

the fishing hut

Glen Loch 3

↑Continued Glen Tilt 6↑

↑Continued Gleann Fearnach 4

←Continued Tarf Water 2 and Glen Tilt 6←

500 m
450 400

River — Tilt

An Lochain

450

550 m

600 m

650 m

450 m

650 m

600 m

500 m

Allt Glen Loch drains to the south east whilst Loch Loch sheds its water north into the Tilt. The flat water-shed is at the foot of this page. The way north to the Tilt is suitable only for walkers. The Tilt is seldom safe to ford.

N 1/km

600 m

Meall a Mhuirich

898 m

718 m

Continued Gleann Fearnach 3↓

Loch Loch

Beinn a Ghlo

650 m 600 m 500 m

722 m

600 m 550 m 500 m

726 m

←Cont'd Glen Loch 1↓   ↓Continued Glen Loch 2↓

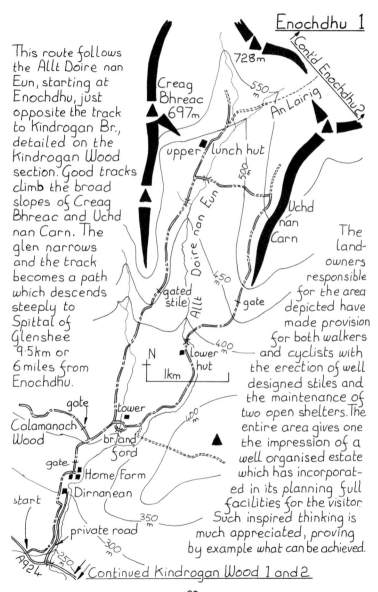

This route follows the Allt Doire nan Eun, starting at Enochdhu, just opposite the track to Kindrogan Br., detailed on the Kindrogan Wood section. Good tracks climb the broad slopes of Creag Bhreac and Uchd nan Carn. The glen narrows and the track becomes a path which descends steeply to Spittal of Glenshee 9.5km or 6 miles from Enochdhu.

The landowners responsible for the area depicted have made provision for both walkers and cyclists with the erection of well designed stiles and the maintenance of two open shelters. The entire area gives one the impression of a well organised estate which has incorporated in its planning full facilities for the visitor. Such inspired thinking is much appreciated, proving by example what can be achieved.

Contd Enochdhu 2

728m

Creag Bhreac 697m

An Lairig

upper lunch hut

Uchd nan Carn

Allt Doire nan Eun

gated stile

gate

N

1km

lower hut

tower

gate

Calamanach Wood

br. and ford

gate

Home Farm

Dirnanean

start

private road

A924

<u>Continued Kindrogan Wood 1 and 2</u>

Enochdhu 2

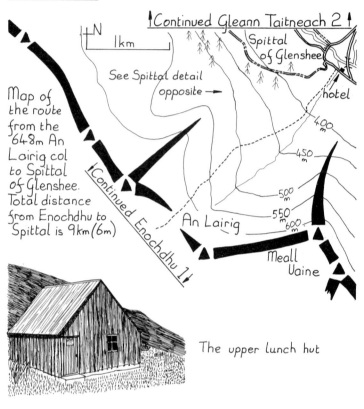

↑Continued Gleann Taitneach 2↑

Spittal of Glenshee

hotel

See Spittal detail opposite →

Map of the route from the 648m An Lairig col to Spittal of Glenshee. Total distance from Enochdhu to Spittal is 9km (6m)

↓Continued Enochdhu 1↓

An Lairig

Meall Uaine

400 m
450 m
500 m
550 m
600 m

The upper lunch hut

The lower hut

The head of Glenshee is a mile or so above Spittal of Glenshee, the Cairnwell road follows Gleann Beag up to the skier's car park which scars the summit. Glenshee then divides into Glen Lochsie and Gleann Taitneach both interesting areas for exploration. Gleann Taitneach, the longer glen, is 'cyclable' to within about a mile below Loch nan Eun. Glen Lochsie has two alternative starting points, both routes converging before the Lodge, and the added interest of an abandoned railway which once carried its passengers from the Dalmunzie Hotel to Glenlochsie Lodge. The track beyond the lodge is an unforgivable scar bulldozed up a mountain spur to assist drainage but offensive to the eyes of all who really appreciate the wild glens.

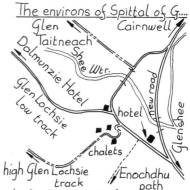

The environs of Spittal of G....

Glen Taitneach · Cairnwell · Dalmunzie Hotel · Shee Wtr. · Glen Lochsie low track · hotel · new road · Glenshee · chalets · high Glen Lochsie track · Enochdhu path

Glenlochsie Lodge, from near the "railway station".

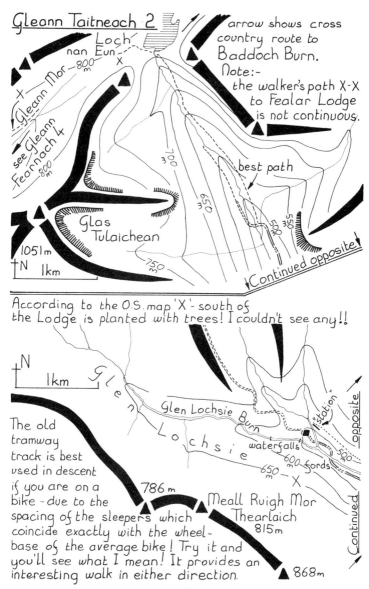

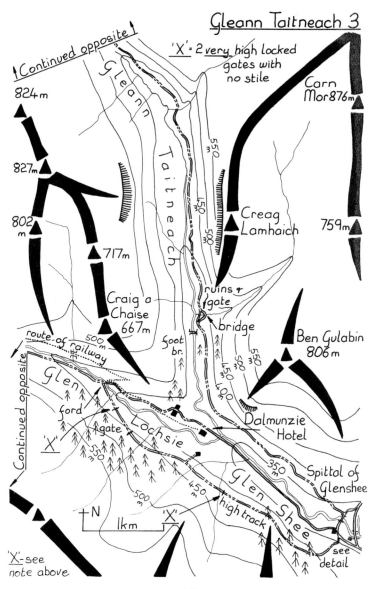

Gleann Taitneach 3

'X' = 2 very high locked gates with no stile

Continued opposite ↑

824 m

Gleann

Carn Mor 876 m

827 m

550

Taitneach

802 m

450 m

717 m

Creag Lamhaich

500 m

759 m

Craig a Chaise 667 m

ruins & gate

bridge

route of railway

500 m

foot br.

450 500 550 m

Ben Gulabin 806 m

Continued opposite

Glen

ford

gate

Lochsie

550 m

500 m

450 m

Dalmunzie Hotel

350 m

Glen Shee

Spittal of Glenshee

high track

N   1km   'X'

see detail

'X' - see note above

Baddoch Burn 1

The Baddoch Burn flows down an un-named and un-remarkable glen from a high wilderness area which is almost connected to both Glen Ey (refer Book 1) and Gleann Taitneach. The end of the track is met after a climb, and other than to enjoy the almost guaranteed solitude or to walk over rough heather to the almost adjoining glens, to pursue the track to the end may seem pointless. However the 7km (4 mile) distance each way makes the return excursion suitable for a half-day or summer evening sortie. The ruined bothy was well used for many years by climbers and walkers whose inscriptions can still be seen on the collapsed walls. Be careful in case a bit more collapses on you!

Note:- The possible through routes via Loch nan Eun and to Glen Ey are pathless and fitness and equipment (and knowledge of its use) should reflect this.

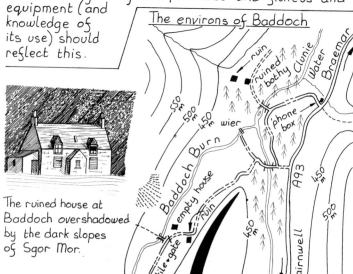

The environs of Baddoch

The ruined house at Baddoch overshadowed by the dark slopes of Sgor Mor.

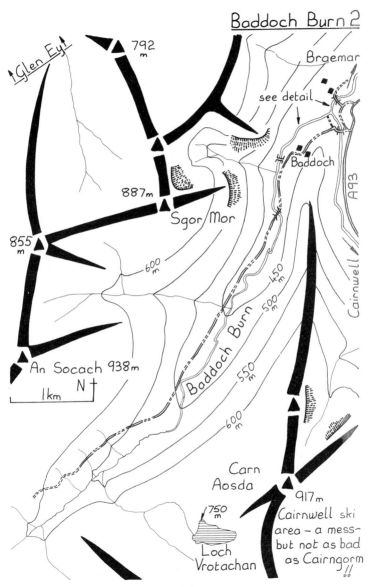

Baddoch Burn 2

792 m

↑Glen Ey↑

Braemar

see detail

Baddoch

887m

A93

Sgor Mor

855 m

600

Cairnwell

450 m

500 m

Baddoch Burn

An Socach 938m

N↑

1km

550 m

600

Carn
Aosda

917m

750 m

Cairnwell ski
area – a mess–
but not as bad
as Cairngorm
!!

Loch
Vrotachan

Aberfeldy to Dunkeld

Access:- Access to the Aberfeldy to Dunkeld area could not be easier. The area lies east and west of the A9 only 20-30 miles north of Perth. Travelling north Dunkeld is reached with Strathbraan to the west leading to Loch Kennard and Loch Hoil. North of Dunkeld lies the Loch Ordie network of tracks. A little further north Strath Tay leads west to Aberfeldy, the northern access to Lochs Kennard and Hoil with the Camserney Burn just beyond the town. East of Pitlochry the A924 leads into Strath Ardle for Kindrogan Wood. Again west of the A9, north of Loch Tummel lies the Tummel Forest, or Glen Fincastle. Dunkeld and Pitlochry have railway stations.

Accommodation:- Plentiful and varied. I need only refer you to the tourist information centres at Aberfeldy Dunkeld and Pitlochry.

Geographical Features:- Very much an area of lochs and forests apart from the wild moors above Loch Ordie. Rather than neatly defined glens the tracks comprise networks of routes. This is an excellent area for those new to mountainbiking as easy high level tracks can be followed for miles, usually with an easy exit to the nearest road. As most routes start in populated areas great respect must be shown for local people, it is their home and their back garden!! Reference to the O.S. map shows many more apparently feasible routes, however many start in private grounds, especially north of Aberfeldy. The routes included on the following pages are tried and tested and provide good coverage of the area without being intrusive.

Mountains:- Not many! Rolling hills make this area different in character from the rest of this guide but this does not detract from either the beauty or the interest of the locality.

Rivers:- The area is dissected by the River Tay - fortunately this does not have to be forded! The River Quaich/Braan flows east to Dunkeld to join the Tay, and the Tummel flows east, then south to join the Tay just south of Ballinluig. The routes given are remarkably free of major fords so if you don't like paddling this area is for you!

Forests:- Tummel Forest and the forests of Loch Kennard cover great tracts of land. Much more planting is taking place at Loch Broom so if you want extensive views be quick - before the trees grow! Many people object to too much forestry but if some moorland is left in between it does provide scenic variety, and miles of tracks, the scars of which are hidden from distant view. There are few natural areas of woodland.

Lochs:- This is an area of lochs. The largest is Loch Tummel, next is the lesser known Loch Freuchie to the south, then Loch of Lowes nature reserve near Dunkeld. However the dozen or so hill lochs provide the best interest of the region. The choice lies between the contouring forest tracks of Loch Kennard and the climb to the various fishing lochs. Above Dunkeld Loch Ordie is surrounded by smaller hill lochs and this network of tracks provides several days walking and at least a couple of days cycling, without covering the same ground twice.

Emergency:- Despite some of the routes being quite long the explorer of these forests and lochs is never very far away from the road. The exception is Loch Ordie - the tracks north of here are very slow going for the mountainbiker and whilst Loch Ordie down to Dunkeld is quick Lochan Oisinneach Beag to Loch Ordie is an entirely different story. Please don't get caught out. The remainder of the glens are too well populated to be a safety problem.

Aberfeldy to Dunkeld Routes 1

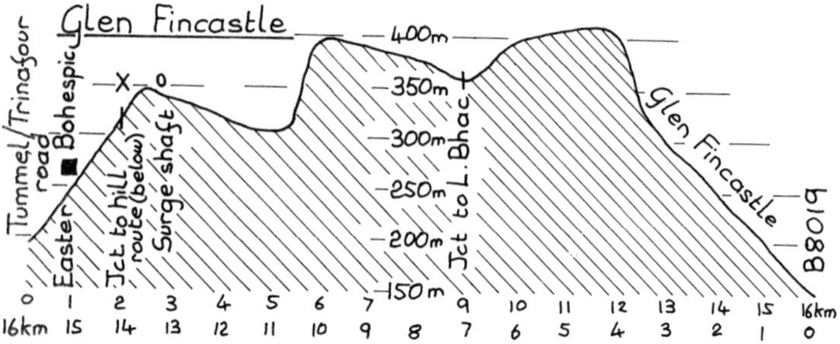
Glen Fincastle
Tummel/Trinafour road
Easter Bohespic
Jct to hill route (below)
X
0
Surge shaft
400m
350m
300m
250m
200m
150m
Jct to L. Bhac
Glen Fincastle
B8019
0 1 2 3 4 5 6 7 9 10 11 12 13 14 15 16km
16km 15 14 13 12 11 10 9 8 7 6 5 4 3 2 1 0

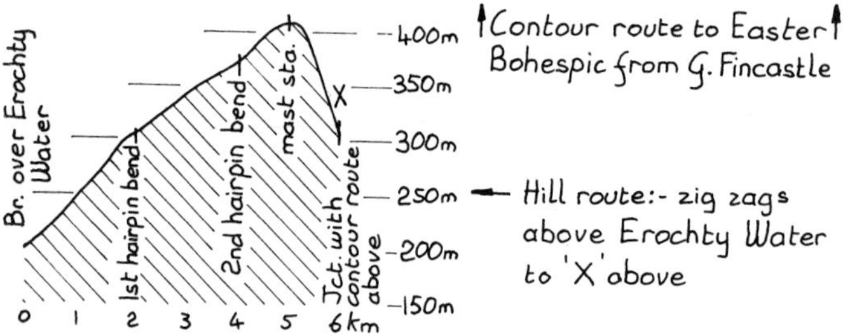
Br. over Erochty Water
1st hairpin bend
2nd hairpin bend
mast sta.
X
Jct. with contour route above
400m
350m
300m
250m
200m
150m
0 1 2 3 4 5 6km
Contour route to Easter Bohespic from G. Fincastle
Hill route:- zig zags above Erochty Water to 'X' above

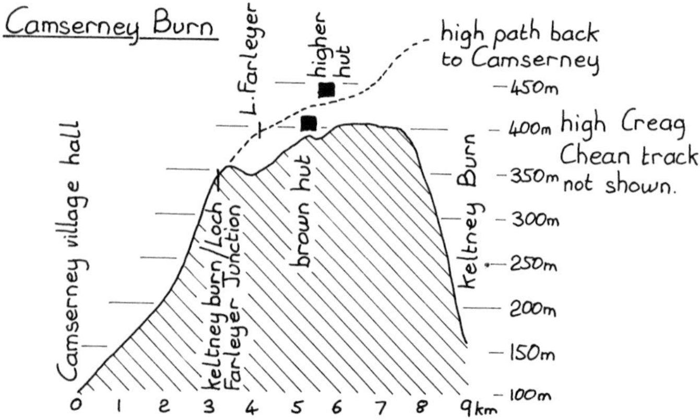
Camserney Burn
L. Farleyer
higher hut
high path back to Camserney
450m
400m
350m
300m
250m
200m
150m
100m
high Creag Chean track not shown.
Camserney village hall
keltney burn/Loch Farleyer Junction
brown hut
keltney Burn
0 1 2 3 4 5 6 7 8 9km

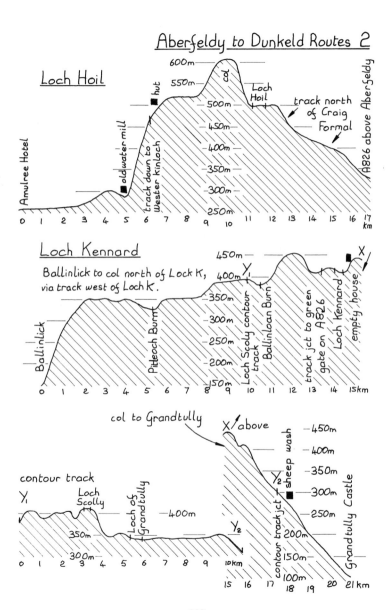

Loch Hoil

Loch Kennard

Ballinlick to col north of Lock K, via track west of Lock K.

col to Grandtully

contour track

105

Aberfeldy to Dunkeld Routes 3

Loch Skaich

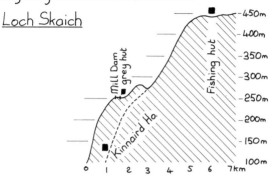

Loch Ordie

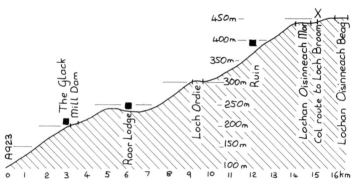

Buckney Burn Link

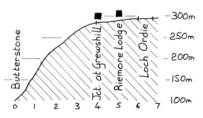

Link to Loch Broom from X

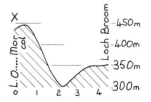

Loch Broom

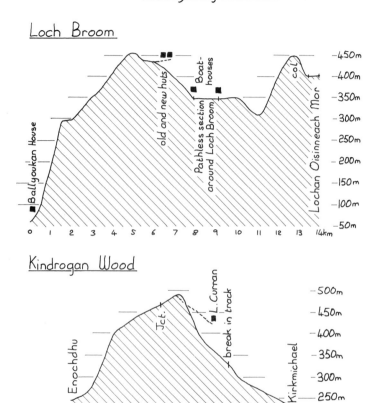

- Ballyoukan House
- old and new huts
- Boat-houses
- Pathless section around Loch Broom
- Lochan Oisinneach Mor
- col

450m
400m
350m
300m
250m
200m
150m
100m
50m

0 1 2 3 4 5 6 7 8 9 10 11 12 13 14km

Kindrogan Wood

- Enochdhu
- Jct.
- L. Curran
- break in track
- Kirkmichael

500m
450m
400m
350m
300m
250m
200m

0 1 2 3 4 5 6 7 8 9 10km

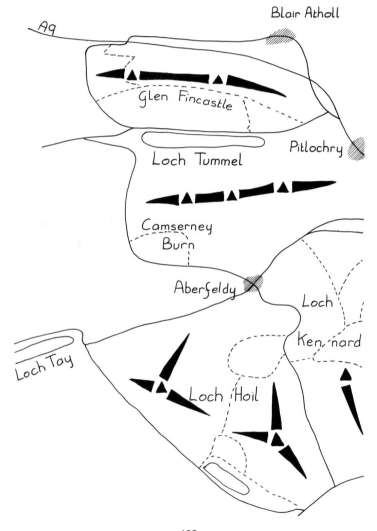

Blair Atholl

A9

Glen Fincastle

Loch Tummel

Pitlochry

Camserney
Burn

Aberfeldy

Loch

Ken nard

Loch Tay

Loch Hoil

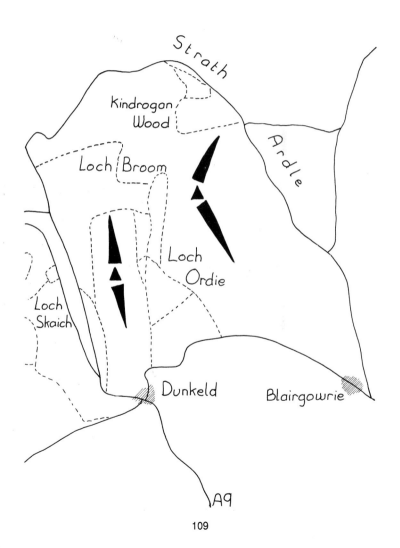

Glen Fincastle 1

This section could have been entitled Tummel Forest but Glen Fincastle sounds better! The glen provides access to some fine high level forest roads and once height is gained the traverse of the forest provides grand views both north to Glen Bruar  and its surrounding heights and south to Schiehallion. The Queen's View forest walks are waymarked short walks from the visitor centre but the walker and cyclist must visit Loch Bhac and traverse the longer routes to fully appreciate all the Forest has to offer. Extended walks need a pre-arranged pick-up point whilst the cyclist may return either by Loch Tummel or Glen Errochty. The October colours of birch and other trees by Loch Tummel are a sight not to be missed! There is shelter at the hut but remember this is private property. The surge shaft is a death trap. Please Mr Hydro-Electric put a lid on it!

Loch Bhac hut

110

Due to the variety of routes possible in the Tummel Forest area the map below allows the distances to be easily calculated in either km or, in brackets, miles.

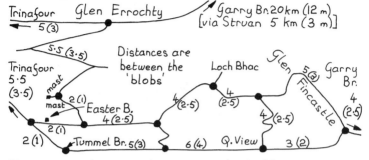

Trinafour   Glen Errochty   Garry Br. 20km (12 m)
← 5(3)   [via Struan 5 km (3 m)]

5·5 (3·5)   Distances are   Loch Bhac   Glen Fincastle   Garry Br.
Trinafour   between the   5 (3)
5·5   'blobs'   4
(3·5)   mast   4 (2·5)   4 (2·5)   (2·5)
         mast   2 (1)   4 (2·5)
         Easter B.
         2 (1)   4 (2·5)
2 (1)   2 (1)   Tummel Br. 5(3)   6 (4)   Q. View   3 (2)

The view north to Glen Bruar from Loch Bhac

Glen Fincastle 3

To Dalnacardoch (see Water)
Edendon

Trinafour

G l e n   E r r o c h t y

The track X-X should be ═══
but due to heavy forestry traffic
when surveyed was ═══
and muddy! ie – hard
work cycling
uphill!

Errochty Water

B847

250 m
300 m
350 m

B847

Big Wood
(you're not
joking!)

X

X

Jct. to
Kinloch Rannoch

512 m

450 m

Tummel

Forest

400

opposite →

General Wades Military Road

350 m

400

300 m

site of old mast
(such a pity no-one
picks up the respons-
ibility of clearing up
the dereliction left
behind)

Continued →

The track
via the farm
of Easter Bohespic
provides one of the
few road links to
the high level route
to Glen Fincastle.

The prominent mountain
just south of here is
Schiehallion, a
magnificent peak
watching over Lochs
Rannoch, Tummel and Tay.

Easter Bohespic

gates   gate

field

250 m

small sign
to Easter B.

200

↑N
├─── 1km

Kinloch Rannoch

B846

B846

Tummel Br.

112

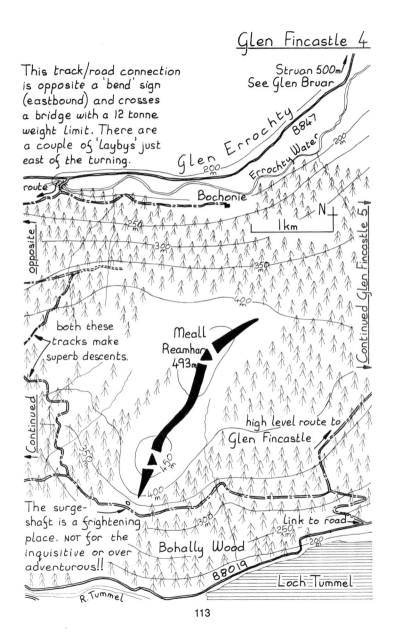

This track/road connection is opposite a 'bend' sign (eastbound) and crosses a bridge with a 12 tonne weight limit. There are a couple of 'laybys' just east of the turning.

Struan 500m
See Glen Bruar

Glen Errochty

B847

Errochty Water

200 m

route

Bochonie

N

1 km

opposite

250

300

350

400

both these tracks make superb descents.

Meall Reamhar 493m

Continued

350

high level route to Glen Fincastle

450 m

400 m

The surge-shaft is a frightening place. NOT for the inquisitive or over adventurous!!

300 m

Bohally Wood

250 m

Link to road

200

B8019

Loch Tummel

R. Tummel

Glen Fincastle 5

The signpost at the start of the short diversion to Loch Bhac. View 'X' is north to Glen Bruar.

LOCH BHAC

NO VEHICLES BEYOND THIS POINT

Loch Bhac is a magical oasis in a desert of trees - perched almost on the hilltop. The 200m diversion to the fishing hut should not be missed.

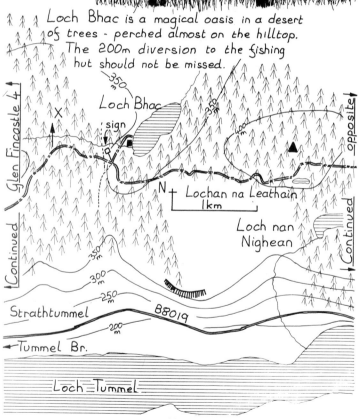

Glen Fincastle 4

Continued

X

350

Loch Bhac

sign

350

300
m

Continued

opposite

N

Lochan na Leathain

1km

Loch nan Nighean

350
m

300
m

250
m

Strathtummel

B8019

200
m

Tummel Br.

Loch Tummel

The environs of Edintian.

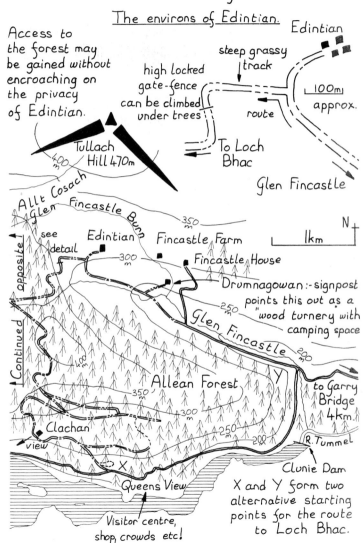

Edintian

steep grassy track

Access to the forest may be gained without encroaching on the privacy of Edintian.

high locked gate-fence can be climbed under trees

route

|100m| approx.

Tullach Hill 470m

400 m

To Loch Bhac

Glen Fincastle

Allt Cosach

Glen Fincastle Burn

350 m

N

1km

see detail

Edintian

Fincastle Farm

300 m

Fincastle House

Drumnagowan :- signpost points this out as a "wood turnery" with camping space

250 m

Glen Fincastle

200

Continued opposite

400 m

Allean Forest

350 m

300 m

Y

to Garry Bridge 4km

Clachan

250 m

200

view

R. Tummel

X

Clunie Dam

Queens View

X and Y form two alternative starting points for the route to Loch Bhac.

Visitor centre, shop, crowds etc!

Camserney Burn 1

The Camserney Burn is a short tributary of the Tay
rising in the upland area of Loch Farleyer and
provides a variety of routes equally suited to both
walker and mountainbiker as distances are generally
short. The beautiful hamlet of Camserney with its
thatched cottages nestles at the start of the
route. Camserney is only 4km or 2.5
miles from the town of Aberfeldy.

Tummel Bridge 7km or 4.5 miles

Creag Chean 654m

N

1km

Contd. opposite

Creag Odhar 523m

Camserney Burn

brown hut

metal gate

No link!

Y: sm. fords

locked deer gate (and stile)

X

X- old milestone ??

475 m

The tracks of Dull Wood were
not surveyed by the author as there
is no link to the Camserney Burn

Keltney Burn

Dull

Keltneyburn

River Lyon

Appin of Dull

116

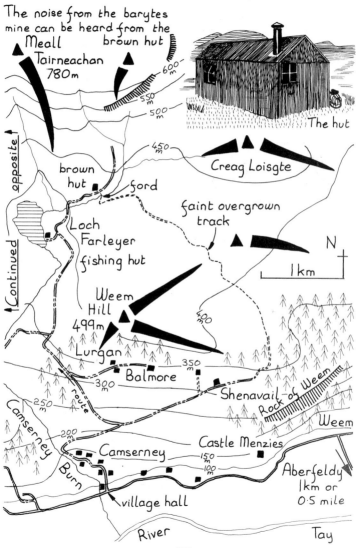

The noise from the barytes mine can be heard from the brown hut

Meall Tairneachan 780m

600m
550m
500m

The hut

opposite↑

Continued ←

450m

brown hut

ford

Loch Farleyer fishing hut

faint overgrown track

Creag Loisgte

N

1km

Weem Hill 499m

400

Lurgan

350m

Balmore

300m

Shenavail

Rock of Weem

Weem

route

250m

200m

Camserney

Castle Menzies

150m

100m

Aberfeldy 1km or 0·5 mile

Camserney Burn

village hall

River

Tay

Loch Hoil 1

Loch Hoil is an unremarkable sheet of water perched up a hillside some 6km or 4 miles south of Aberfeldy. A new track, an unfortunate scar until 'weathered', links the woodland tracks of Loch Hoil with Glen Quaich and Amulree. The hillsides around Craig Formal had an uncommonly high population of barn owls when the area was surveyed by the author.

the shed

high locked gate
+stile

Aberfeldy 3·5km

pylons

sheep wash
small ford

Elrig Mhor

Quarry

400 m

Craig Formal
▲ 511m

N

1 km

stile

350

Loch
na
Creige

green gate
Continued Loch Kennard 3

500 m

450 m

Monadh
nam Mial
▲ 604m

high
locked
gate and
stile

350

high locked gate
(no stile)

locked shed

boathouse

Loch
Hoil

500 m

high gate
and stile

430

↓ Continued Loch Hoil 2 ↓

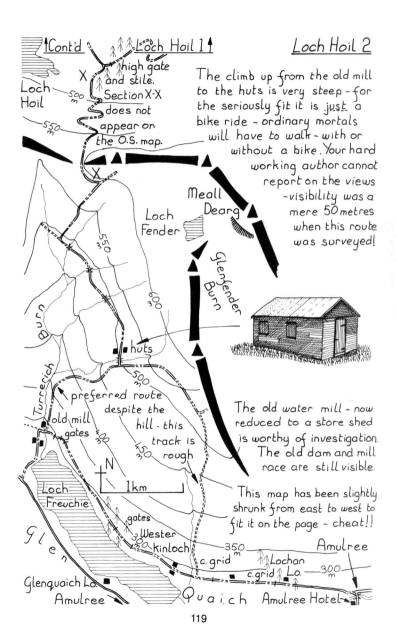

Loch Hoil 2

↑high gate and stile. Section X-X does not appear on the O.S. map.

Loch Hoil

500 m

550 m

X

X

Meall Dearg

Loch Fender

Glenfender Burn

Turrerich Burn

550 m

600 m

500 m

huts

preferred route despite the hill - this track is rough

450 m

300 m

old mill

gates

N

1km

Loch Freuchie

gates

Wester kinloch

300 m

c. grid

350 m

Lochan Lo.

c. grid

300 m

Amulree

Glen

Quaich

Glenquaich Lo.

Amulree

Amulree Hotel

The climb up from the old mill to the huts is very steep - for the seriously fit it is just a bike ride - ordinary mortals will have to walk - with or without a bike. Your hard working author cannot report on the views - visibility was a mere 50 metres when this route was surveyed!

The old water mill - now reduced to a store shed is worthy of investigation. The old dam and mill race are still visible.

This map has been slightly shrunk from east to west to fit it on the page - cheat!!

119

Loch Kennard 1

The forest roads of Loch Kennard provide numerous high level routes contouring around Grandtully Hill and Creag a Mhadaidh. A through route gives an off-road ride or walk from Dunkeld to Aberfeldy. The tracks are generally good and access to Loch Kennard is possible from Ballintick 5km west of Dunkeld; from two points on the A827 between Aberfeldy and Grandtully; and from the green gate near Loch na Craige on the Glen Cochill road, see Loch Hoil 1. There is no connection to Craigvinean Forest (which is not included in this book as it comprises an unremarkable set of forest tracks all on the same hillside above the noisy A9) nor is there a connection to the track rising from Sketewan on the B898. Both the above appear as routes on the O.S. Pathfinder maps but a couple of afternoons spent investigating these possibilities by yours truly only revealed dead-ends and firebreaks. Loch Kennard drains into the Ballinloan Burn which feeds the River Braan as it descends from Amulree to the River Tay at Inver, just outside Dunkeld.

The forlorn boarded-up house just above Loch Kennard - it seems such a waste!

The Hermitage

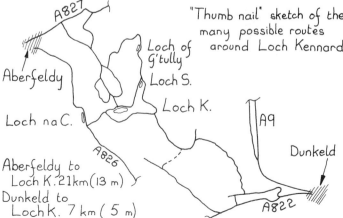

"Thumb nail' sketch of the many possible routes around Loch Kennard

A827

Aberfeldy

Loch of G'tully

Loch S.

Loch K.

Loch na C.

A826

A9

Dunkeld

Aberfeldy to Loch K. 21km (13 m)

Dunkeld to Loch K. 7 km (5 m)

A822

121

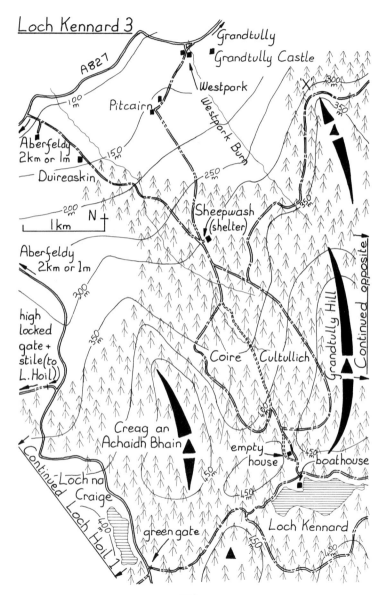

Loch Kennard 3

A827

Grandtully
Grandtully Castle

Westpark

Pitcairn

100 m

Westpark Burn

Aberfeldy
2km or 1m

150 m

Duireaskin

250 m

Sheepwash
(shelter)

200 m

300 m

1km N

Aberfeldy
2km or 1m

350 m

high
locked
gate +
stile (to
L. Hoil)

350 m

Coire   Cultullich

Creag an
Achaidh Bhain

empty
house

150 m

boathouse

Grandtully Hill

Continued opposite

Continued Loch Hoil 1

Loch na
Craige

400 m

green gate

150 m

150 m

Loch Kennard

150 m

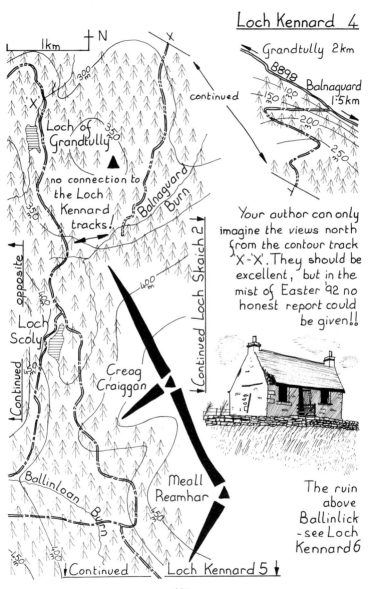

1km

N

Grandtully 2km

B898

Balnaguard 1·5km

continued

300m

Loch of Grandtully

350

no connection to the Loch Kennard tracks!

Balnaguard Burn

100

150

200m

250m

Your author can only imagine the views north from the contour track 'X'-'X'. They should be excellent, but in the mist of Easter '92 no honest report could be given!!

350

400m

opposite

Loch Skaich 2

Continued

Loch Scoly

Creag Craiggan

Continued

Ballinloan Burn

Meall Reamhar

150

The ruin above Ballinlick –see Loch Kennard 6

150

150

Continued

Loch Kennard 5 ↓

123

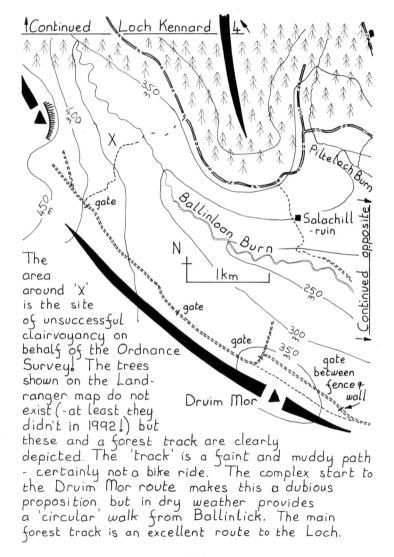

↑Continued   Loch Kennard 4↑

350 m

400
350

X

450 m

gate

Ballinloan Burn

Pilteloch Burn

■ Salachill
-ruin

N

1km

250 m

gate

gate

300 m
350 m

gate
between
fence &
wall

gate

Druim Mor

Continued opposite

The area around 'X' is the site of unsuccessful clairvoyancy on behalf of the Ordnance Survey! The trees shown on the Land-ranger map do not exist (-at least they didn't in 1992!) but these and a forest track are clearly depicted. The 'track' is a faint and muddy path - certainly not a bike ride. The complex start to the Druim Mor route makes this a dubious proposition, but in dry weather provides a 'circular' walk from Ballinlick. The main forest track is an excellent route to the Loch.

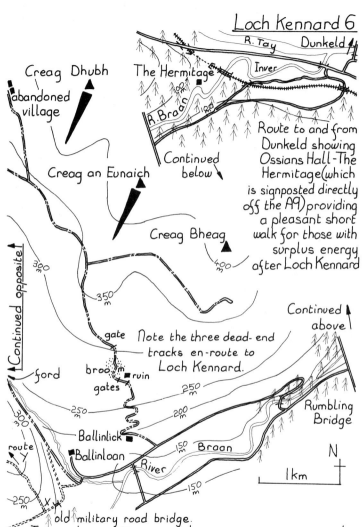

R. Tay

Dunkeld

The Hermitage

Inver

Creag Dhubh

abandoned village

R. Broan

Continued below ↓

Route to and from Dunkeld showing Ossians Hall-The Hermitage(which is signposted directly off the A9) providing a pleasant short walk for those with surplus energy after Loch Kennard

Creag an Eunaich

Creag Bheag

400m

300m

350m

Continued above ↑

Continued opposite ↑

gate

broo ruin

gates

Note the three dead-end tracks en-route to Loch Kennard.

250m

200m

Rumbling Bridge

ford

300m

250m

Ballinlick

150m

Braan

route Y

Ballinloan

River

N

1 km

250m

X

150m

old military road bridge.

To reach point X across the vague grassy approach head for the top corner of the wood(which becomes a row of trees). The route Y may be seen on the right up steep grass. This route is more obvious downhill.

125

Loch Skaich 1

The track up to the fishing lodge at Loch Skaich is best approached via the track starting opposite the entrance to Kinnaird House. The branch track to Mill Dam has been recently improved. The remaining tracks are becoming overgrown with heather though still passable. Tracks becoming overgrown in this way possibly reduce the overall effect of new tracks being bulldozed, often without planning permission, all over Scotland, but bulldozing is so rapid (and unsightly), and it takes about 20 years or more for a new track to become overgrown and visually acceptable. Many more years of disuse are needed before a track begins to return, as those around Loch Skaich – to wild moorland. I digress, the track to the fishing lodge makes a good half day or evening short excursion. Only 3km (1.5 miles) and a low watershed separate Loch Skaich from Loch Kennard but the connection is pathless and barred by deer fence and trees before the Loch Kennard tracks are reached.

descent via birchwood

gate
stone sheep pen

x y   boggy

Detail at
Mill Dam

tracks X and Y converge into the same dead end!

Loch S.

Mill Dam   grey hut

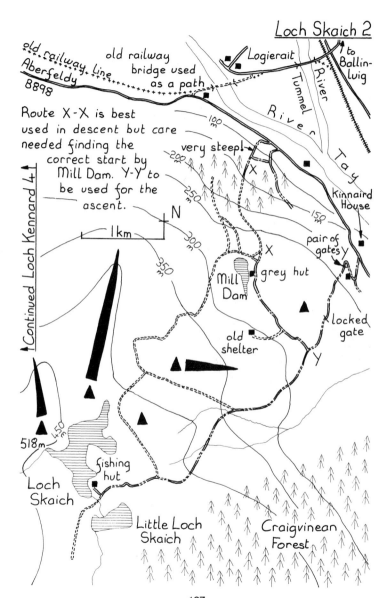

Loch Skaich 2

old railway line
Aberfeldy
B898

old railway
bridge used
as a path

Logierait

to Ballin-luig

River Tummel

River Tay

Route X-X is best
used in descent but care
needed finding the
correct start by
Mill Dam. Y-Y to
be used for the
ascent.

very steep!

X

100

200

250 m

150 m

Kinnaird House

pair of gates

Continued Loch Kennard 4

1km

N

300

350 m

X

Mill Dam

grey hut

old shelter

locked gate

Y

518m

450 m

Loch Skaich

fishing hut

Little Loch Skaich

Craigvinean Forest

127

Loch Ordie 1

Loch Ordie and its environs provides an excellent variety of mountainbiking and walking routes starting almost from the very centre of Dunkeld. Easy forest and moorland tracks lead up to the loch and rougher, more demanding tracks probe far into an area of moorland which feels truly wild despite close proximity to Strath Tay and the A9. An exciting through route via Loch Broom is possible to the north. Access to and from the area is possible from the Buckney Burn and several points in Strath Tay. However, a word of warning, several of the approach routes which seem possible on the O.S. map are rather intrusive and these are identified on the following pages. (I ended up almost on the lawn at Riemore Lodge after descending from the hill!) Remember no-one has the right to tramp or cycle over someone else's property, your good manners, and respect of the quite reasonable wish of local people for peace and privacy will allow access to continue. Ask permission where you can and apologise if you have to! Close study of the O.S. map and these pages is needed before setting off. The area drains into the rivers Tay, Ardle and Ericht. Shelter is available at Mill Dam boathouse (room for 200!); the ruin (just - and probably not for long); and the "tin hut".

Lochordie
  Lodge

128

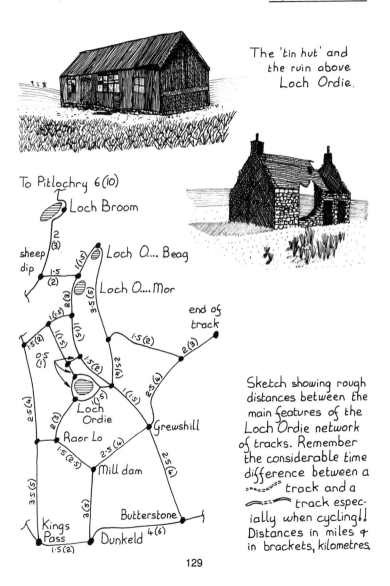

The 'tin hut' and
the ruin above
Loch Ordie.

To Pitlochry 6(10)

Loch Broom

2 (3)

sheep dip

1.5 (2)

Loch O.... Beag

1 (1.5)

Loch O.... Mor

2 (3)

3.5 (5)

1 (1.5)

1.5 (2)

1 (1.5)

5 (1)

end of track

1.5 (2)

2 (3)

0.5 (1)

1.5 (2)

2.5 (4)

1 (1.5)

2.5 (4)

Loch Ordie

1 (1.5)

2.5 (4)

Raor Lo

2 (3)

Grewshill

2.5 (4)

1.5 (2.5)

2.5 (4)

Mill dam

2.5 (4)

3.5 (5)

3 (5)

Butterstone

Kings Pass

1.5 (2)

Dunkeld

4 (6)

Sketch showing rough
distances between the
main features of the
Loch Ordie network
of tracks. Remember
the considerable time
difference between a
===== track and a
===== track espec-
ially when cycling!!
Distances in miles &
in brackets, kilometres.

129

Loch Ordie 3

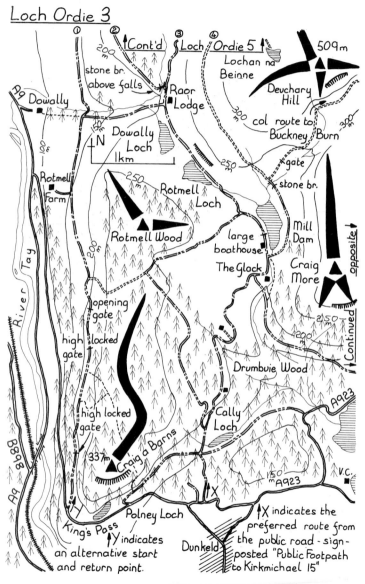

① ② ↑ Cont'd ③ ④ Loch Ordie 5 ↑

509m

Lochan na Beinne

stone br. above falls

Deuchary Hill

Raor Lodge

col route to Buckney Burn

A9 Dowally

gate

Dowally Loch

250m

stone br.

N 1km

Rotmell Loch

Mill Dam

Rotmell Farm

Rotmell Wood

250m

Craig More

large boathouse

The Glack

200m

opening gate

150m

high locked gate

Drumbuie Wood

200m

A923

high locked gate

Cally Loch

337m Craig a Barns

150m A923

V.C.

King's Pass

Polney Loch

X indicates the preferred route from the public road - sign-posted "Public Footpath to Kirkmichael 15"

Y indicates an alternative start and return point.

Dunkeld

River Tay

B898 A9

100m

200m

300m

300m

Continued ↓

opposite →

130

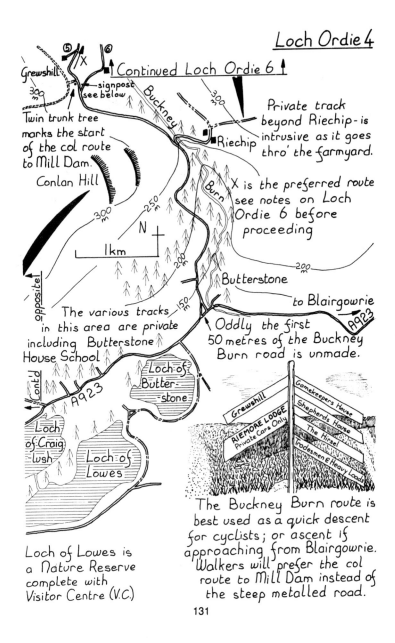

Grewshill

⑤ ✗ ⑥

300 m

← signpost see below

↑ Continued Loch Ordie 6 ↑

Buckney

300 m

Riechip

Private track beyond Riechip - is intrusive as it goes thro' the farmyard.

Twin trunk tree marks the start of the col route to Mill Dam. Conlan Hill

250 m

Burn

300 m

✗ is the preferred route see notes on Loch Ordie 6 before proceeding

N

1km

200 m

Butterstone

150 m

to Blairgowrie

A923

← opposite!

The various tracks in this area are private including Butterstone House School

Oddly the first 50 metres of the Buckney Burn road is unmade.

Cont'd

A923

Loch of Butter-stone

Loch of Craig Lush

Loch of Lowes

Grewshill

RIEMORE LODGE Private Cars Only

Gamekeepers House

Shepherds House

The Hirsel

Tradesmen & Heavy Loads

The Buckney Burn route is best used as a quick descent for cyclists; or ascent if approaching from Blairgowrie. Walkers will prefer the col route to Mill Dam instead of the steep metalled road.

Loch of Lowes is a Nature Reserve complete with Visitor Centre (V.C.)

131

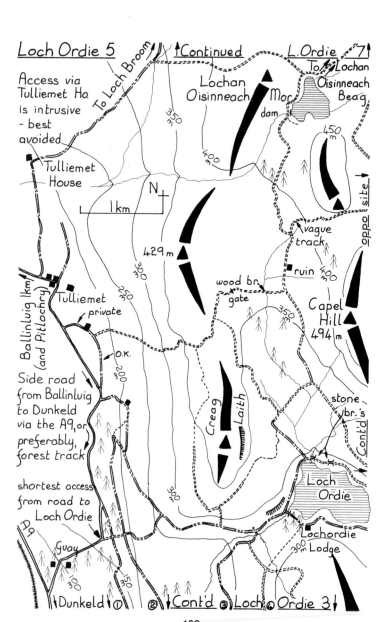

↑Continued

To Lochan
Oisinneach
Beag

Lochan
Oisinneach Mor

dam

Access via
Tulliemet Ho.
is intrusive
– best
avoided

To Loch Broom

350

450
m

400

Tulliemet
House

oppo site →

N

1km

429 m

vague
track

ruin

400

Ballinluig 1km
(and Pitlochry)

Tulliemet
private

300
350

250

wood br.

gate

350

Capel
Hill
494 m

o.k.

300

Side road
from Ballinluig
to Dunkeld
via the A9, or
preferably,
forest track

Creag

Laith

stone
brs.

Cont'd

shortest access
from road to
Loch Ordie

Loch
Ordie

A9

Guay

300
320

Lochordie
Lodge

300
m

150
300

150
300

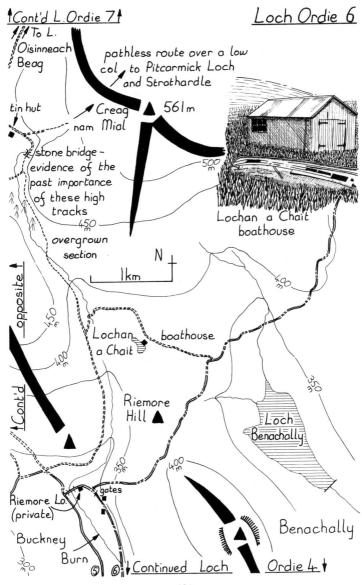

↗↑To L.
Oisinneach
Beag

pathless route over a low
col to Pitcormick Loch
and Strathardle

▲ 561m

tin hut

↗ Creag
nam Mial

stone bridge –
evidence of the
past importance
of these high
tracks

500 m

Lochan a Chait
boathouse

450 m

overgrown
section

N

1km

450

400

400

opposite

Lochan
a Chait ▲   boathouse

Cont'd

Riemore
Hill ▲

350

Loch
Benachally

▲

350

350

Riemore Lo.
(private)

gates

400

Buckney
Burn

300 m

⑤ ⑥ ↓Continued Loch

Benachally

Ordie 4↓

▲

133

Loch Ordie 7

The link route via Loch Broom necessitates a walk around the shore of the loch between the two boathouses. The track from the sheep dip is hard going uphill and the long route around Lochan Oisinneach Beag from and returning to Dunkeld (40km, 25 miles) must not be underestimated.

↑Continued Loch Broom↑

high locked gate + stile
Loch Broom

G l e n   D e r b y

N

1km

502m

Lochbroom Burn

plank br.

Allt Ruighe an Lagain

Meall Reamhar   534m

Lochan Oisinneach Beag

sheep dip

350

400

450

rough, steep grass track

350

300

dam

Lochan O.... Mor

450

Tulliemet House (private)

↓Continued Loch Ordie 5 and 6↓

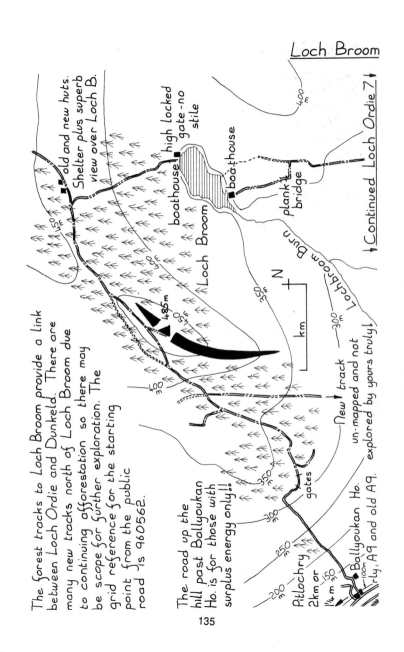

The forest tracks to Loch Broom provide a link between Loch Ordie and Dunkeld. There are many new tracks north of Loch Broom due to continuing afforestation so there may be scope for further exploration. The grid reference for the starting point from the public road is 960562.

The road up the hill past Ballyoukan Ho. is for those with surplus energy only!!

old and new huts.
Shelter plus superb view over Loch B.

boathouse — high locked gate - no stile

boathouse

plank bridge

Loch Broom

Lochbroom Burn

N

km

350 m

300 m

New track — unmapped and not explored by yours truly!

100 m

450 m

485 m

400 m

350 m

300 m

250 m

200 m

150 m

gates

Ballyoukan Ho.

rly, A9 and old A9.

Pitlochry 2km or 1¼ km

400 m

Continued Loch Ordie 7↓

135

Kindrogan Wood 1

Kindrogan Wood comprises an unremarkable set of forest tracks. However, Loch Curran makes a worthwhile objective with its island teeming with nesting black headed gulls in the spring. The best start is from Enochdhu as approach from Kirkmichael is confusing due to the number of driveways to the turf-roofed houses above Log Cabin Hotel.

↑Continued Glen Fearnach 2↑

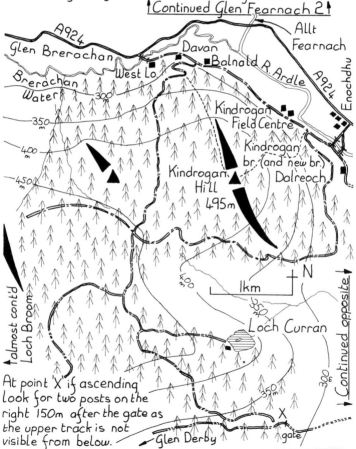

At point 'X' if ascending look for two posts on the right 150m after the gate as the upper track is not visible from below.

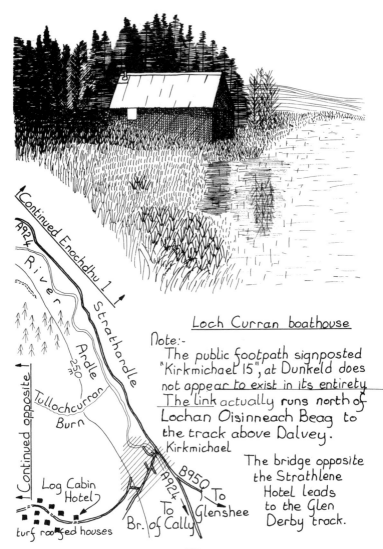

Loch Curran boathouse

Note:-
The public footpath signposted
"Kirkmichael 15", at Dunkeld does
not appear to exist in its entirety.
The link actually runs north of
Lochan Oisinneach Beag to
the track above Dalvey.

The bridge opposite
the Strathlene
Hotel leads
to the Glen
Derby track.

Map labels:

Continued Enochdhu 1

A924

River Ardle

Strathardle

250

Tullochcurran Burn

Continued opposite 1

Log Cabin Hotel

turf roofed houses

Kirkmichael

B950 To Glenshee

A924 To Br. of Cally

Link Routes

The link routes shown demonstrate how the long through routes are made up from the various page maps. Variations can be planned using further adjacent routes but these should provide a basis for extended exploration.

Cuaich/Tromie/Edendon Water

Dalnacardoch

Link Route 1

Glen F'dale 3

Glen Tromie 2

Glen F'dale 2

Glen Tromie 3

Loch Cuaich 2   Loch C.3

Glen Tromie 4

Loch Cuaich 1

Glen Tromie 5

Total distance approx 38km or 24 miles from Kingussie to Dalnacardoch. Don't forget the ford depicted on Glen Tromie 5 !! Dangerous in spate - very wet at best, you have been warned!

Edendon Wtr. 4

Edendon Wtr. 3

Glen Fernisdale to Loch Cuaich via Phones is an off road option to the A9 from Kingussie to Dalwhinnie

Sronphadruig Lodge

35km

30km

Loch Loch an Duin

25km

Loch Bhrodainn

20km

Gaick Lo.

15km

Seilich dam

300m 250m 200m

10km

500m 450m 400m 350m

5km

KINGUSSIE   0

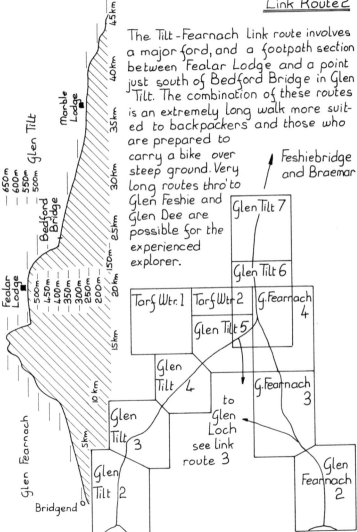

The Tilt-Fearnach link route involves a major ford, and a footpath section between Fealar Lodge and a point just south of Bedford Bridge in Glen Tilt. The combination of these routes is an extremely long walk more suited to backpackers and those who are prepared to carry a bike over steep ground. Very long routes thro' to Glen Feshie and Glen Dee are possible for the experienced explorer.

Feshiebridge and Braemar

Glen Tilt 7

Glen Tilt 6

Tarf Wtr. 1   Tarf Wtr. 2   G. Fearnach 4

Glen Tilt 5

Glen Tilt 4

to Glen Loch see link route 3

Glen Tilt 3

G. Fearnach 3

Glen Tilt 2

Glen Fearnach 2

Bridgend

Glen Fearnach

Marble Lodge

Glen Tilt

Bedford Bridge

Fealar Lodge

650m 600m 550m 500m

500m 450m 400m 350m 300m 250m 200m 150m

45km 40km 35km 30km 25km 20km 15km 10km 5km

139

Glens Fender/Girnaig to Gleann Fearnach

Link Route 3

The link route below is somewhat less demanding than those depicted on the last two pages but still gives the opportunity to explore several glens in one day without being super-fit or spending nights out in the wild. Glen Girnaig is a slow climb, Glen Fender is a better option if cycling from the Blair Atholl end. The route is much quicker and easier starting from Gleann Fearnach. There are no major fords but route finding over the col and around Shinagag requires some care.

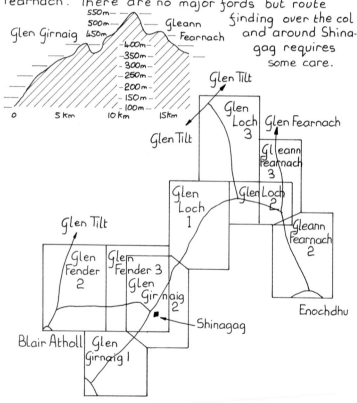

Book 2 complete! Now it's off to Rannoch Moor, but firstly I must thank my publishers for all their help and encouragement, and you dear reader for supporting me by buying Book 1 (I hope), and Book 2. The aim now is to produce a series, and this will only be possible with your continued support – plus enormous amounts of my time researching and writing. What started as little more than a personal record may well develop into a mass of detailed information for the mountainbiker, backpacker and walker. The unruly element referred to at the end of Book 1 seems to be diminishing as far as mountainbiking is concerned, and many people are taking up the sport in a responsible way. Good conduct is essential in retaining access to the tracks and paths of Scotland.... I have personally enjoyed best the wilder areas of The Atholl Glens – Glen Tilt, Glen Fearnach and those routes east of Drumochter that are so easily by-passed on the A9. Blair Atholl has something for everyone, at all standards of fitness. The Aberfeldy to Dunkeld region, whilst providing interest, and good routes for those less experienced or with children, rarely provides complete wilderness and is populated to the extent that one has to exercise care, and respect the privacy of local people, in route selection, as the difference between track and private drive can be subtle. Book 3 - to be based around Rannoch Moor (" The Glens of Rannoch") promises to be an exciting area both for the long distance backpacker and mountainbiker, certainly not an area for the novice! It is to this area that my efforts are now directed - the wild glens and open moor provide an exciting prospect for the next year or so, and if I survive it (!) you too can look forward to reading about and experiencing this unique and extensive region.

THIS BRIDGE WAS ERECTED IN 1886
WITH FUNDS CONTRIBUTED BY
HIS FRIENDS AND OTHERS AND BY
THE SCOTTISH RIGHTS OF WAY SOCIETY LTD
TO COMMEMORATE THE DEATH OF
FRANCIS JOHN BEDFORD, AGED 18
WHO WAS DROWNED NEAR HERE
ON 25TH AUGUST 1879